2750

KRITSMAN
AND THE
AGRARIAN MARXISTS

KRITSMAN
AND THE
AGRARIAN MARXISTS

Edited by
Terry Cox and Gary Littlejohn

FRANK CASS

First published 1984 in Great Britain by
FRANK CASS AND COMPANY LIMITED
Gainsborough House, 11 Gainsborough Road,
London E11 1RS

and in the United States of America by
FRANK CASS AND COMPANY LIMITED
c/o Biblio Distribution Center
81 Adams Drive, P.O.Box 327, Totowa, N.J. 07511

British Library Cataloguing in Publication Data

Kritsman and the Agrarian Marxists.
   1. Kritsman, L.N.   2. Peasantry—Soviet Union
   I. Cox, Terry   II. Littlejohn, Gary
   307.7'2'0947   HD1536.R9

   ISBN 0-7146-3237-6

Library of Congress Cataloging in Publication Data

Main entry under title:
Kritsman and the Agrarian Marxists.

   (The Journal of peasant studies ; v. 11, no.2)
   Bibliography: p.
   1. Peasantry—Soviet Union—History. 2. Social
classes—Soviet Union—History. 3. Agriculture and
state—Soviet Union—History. 4. Soviet Union—Rural
conditions. 5. Kritsman, L. (Lev), 1890–1938. I. Cox,
Terry. II. Littlejohn, Gary. III. Series.
HD1513.A3J68 vol. 11, no. 2   305.5'63s   83–25225
[HD1536.S65]   [305.5'63]
ISBN 0-7146-3237-6

This group of studies first appeared in a Special Issue on
'Kritsman and the Agrarian Marxists' of *The Journal of Peasant
Studies,* Vol. 11, No. 2, published by Frank Cass & Co. Ltd.

Printed in Great Britain by
John Wright and Sons (Printing) Ltd,
at The Stonebridge Press, Bristol

Contents

Editors' Note

The scholarly work on the countryside done in pre-1917 Russia and in the Soviet Union in the 1920s was of a remarkably high quality: of a higher quality, probably, than that on the peasantry of any country before or since. In that corpus, perhaps least known is the work of L. N. Kritsman and those influenced by him – the so-called 'Agrarian Marxists'. Yet the quality of that work was extremely high and it was very original. Moreover, its significance is more than historical, since it has great relevance to the study of peasantries in contemporary poor countries and especially to the analysis of peasant differentiation.

This special issue will help dispel ignorance of this important body of writing. It has been prepared by two guest editors, Terry Cox and Gary Littlejohn, both of whom are specialists on the Soviet Union and both of whom have been working on Kritsman and the Agrarian Marxists for several years. Here they share the results of that work in three major pieces: the first, by Cox, a detailed account of the work of Kritsman and his school; the second, on the political context of the work of the Agrarian Marxists and on the significance of determining the nature of the class structure in the Soviet Union in the 1920s; and the third, an abridged translation of one of Kritsman's important works, *Class Stratification of the Soviet Countryside*.

T. B. BYRES
C. A. CURWEN

Glossary and Abbreviations

Artel	an association or collective of producers, made up of craftsmen or peasants
Barshchina	a system of feudal forced labour required from peasants by landowners
Batrak	agricultural wage labourer
Bednyak	poor peasant
CPSU	Communist Party of the Soviet Union
CW	Collected Works
Desyatin	a measurement of area: 1 *desyatin* = 1.09 hectares = 2.7 acres
Dvor	peasant household
Gosplan	State Planning Commission
Guberniya	province
Khozyain	head of the household
Khutor	a farmstead, physically separated from a village, and not subject to communal repartition
Kolkhoz	collective farm
Kombedy	Committees of Poor Peasants
Kulak	rich peasant, usually hiring labour
Mir	peasant community; government of the community
Narkomtrud	Peoples' Commissariat of Labour
NEP	New Economic Policy
Oblast	largest administrative unit of local government after 1929 when it replaced the *guberniya*
Obshchina	commune
Okrug	subdivision of the *oblast*
Otrub	consolidated farm land, outside the village, and not subject to communal repartition, but without the farm-house which remained inside the village
Promysly	crafts, trades or outside work producing an income
Rabkrin	Peoples' Commissariat of Workers' and Peasants' Inspection
Raion	subdivision of *okrug* and *oblast*
RSDLP	Russian Social Democratic Labour Party
RSFSR	Russian Soviet Federal Socialist Republic
Serednyak	middle peasant
Smychka	alliance between the working class and peasants
S.R.s.	The Socialist Revolutionary Party
Ts.S.U.	Central Statistical Administration
Tyaglo	team of draught animals and ploughman
Uezd	subdivision of the *guberniya*
Volost'	subdivision of the *uezd*
Vserabotzemles	All-Russian Union of Agricultural and Forestry Workers
V.S.N. Kh.	Supreme Council of the National Economy
Zazhitochnye	well-off peasant
Zemstvo	institution of local government in the pre-Revolutionary Russian countryside at *guberniya* or *uezd* levels

Introduction

Terry Cox*

This special issue is devoted to the work of L. N. Kritsman and his colleagues on the question of the class analysis of the Russian peasantry in the 1920s. Although this work is little known today, it is of great interest both for the history of the Russian peasantry and discussion of the problems of attempting socialist construction in the early Soviet countryside, and also for the insights it offers for the theory and methodology of modern studies of peasant class relations. Not only does the work of Kritsman and his colleagues offer a more sophisticated approach to the study of peasant differentiation than has been provided by most other researchers, but also much of the modern debate on this issue has taken place under the influence of Russian works, especially of Lenin on the one hand and Chayanov on the other, without reference to the further work of the Kritsman group which sought to deal with the problems raised by their theories and methods.

In assessing the rural research of Kritsman and those influenced by him, the context of his career and wider interests is very important. Given his position as a Marxist theorist and an active party worker, the aim of his rural research was not simply a description of aspects of peasant life and agriculture, nor was it an attempt to construct a general theory of peasant society as can be found, for example, in Chayanov's work. Rather Kritsman's aim, in the tradition of Marx and Lenin, was to provide a theoretical analysis of the trends in the class character of the Russian peasantry in a particular social formation at a given point in history.[1]

To this end, Kritsman was appointed director of the Agrarian Section of the Soviet Communist Academy in 1925 at a time when the Soviet government was beginning to clearly recognise a growing problem of the growth of capitalist relations in the countryside. Kritsman attracted a group of younger Marxist scholars, most of whom were his juniors by about seven or eight years. They were the first generation of post-graduates after the revolution. Two of them had a background in history and came to the Agrarian Section from the historical section of the Institute of Red Professors. These were A. Gaister and M. Kubanin. Several others, I. Vermenichev, Yu. A. Anisimov, K. Naumov, M. Sulkovskii had been graduates of the Institute of Agricultural Economics of the Timiryazev Academy where they would have been taught by Chayanov and other members of the Organisation and Production School. Together this group became the Agrarian Marxists.[2]

The major theoretical impetus to the group was given by Kritsman in a number of works on the peasantry and the question of class differentiation, beginning in 1925. In a series of articles in 1925, which were expanded into a

*Paisley College of Technology

book in 1926, he carried out an extensive review of all the existing research on the Soviet countryside from which any information on peasant differentiation could be gleaned. On the basis of the available information, Kritsman argued that a new process of class differentiation was taking place in the Russian peasantry of the 1920s, although it was occurring in novel and unexpected ways which the standard statistical approaches did not reflect very well. His work therefore also involved a critique of existing approaches and a plea for the development of a new methodology.

His ideas were first taken up in the formulation of empirical research by V. S. Nemchinov, a statistician working in the Urals, who was not strictly part of the group although he was influenced by Kritsman. Building on Kritsman's ideas and the practical lead of Nemchinov, a number of research projects were carried out by the group on the question of the class differentiation of the peasantry. These studies took the form of surveys of peasant households in chosen areas of the Soviet Union, all using a general questionnaire covering all the households in a given local area, and some also collecting more detailed accounts of peasant budgets from smaller samples of households. There were also some studies which analysed data from several different areas which had been collected by the Central Statistical Bureau (Ts. S. U.) of the Soviet Union.

Towards the end of the 1920s the Agrarian Marxists were beginning to make an impact. Their influence was growing at the expense of rival schools of thought in agrarian research such as that of Chayanov and his colleagues, and their ideas were gradually being accepted for new approaches in rural social research, in the collection of agrarian statistics, and in the development of an agronomy which would be sensitive to class differences between peasant farms. However, with the forced collectivisation of the peasants at the end of the 1920s, in which peasants were categorised into social classes in a highly arbitrary manner by state officials, the research of the Agrarian Marxists came to be regarded as superfluous or even politically dangerous by the state. From 1930 no more research was carried out by the group. Kritsman and his colleagues quickly lost much of their influence, then their jobs, and by the end of the 1930s most of them had lost their lives.

As far as their research was concerned, the Agrarian Marxists left behind a body of work which, while unfinished, and ultimately inconclusive in fulfilling its aim of a detailed analysis of the Soviet rural social structure as a whole, was nevertheless highly productive of a number of interesting ideas about the nature of the peasantry and about ways of studying them. These remain useful both for a retrospective look at the Soviet Union of the 1920s, and for adaptation to the study of peasantries in other parts of the world today. For modern historians, both in the Soviet Union and in the West, the work of the Kritsman school has been a vital source of insights and information about the Soviet Union of the 1920s. However, while much historical research remains to be done, for which the research of the Agrarian Marxists would prove useful, the main aim here is to introduce the theoretical, methodological and political contributions of the Kritsman school as a particularly interesting example of an attempt at a Marxist social science of the peasantry. This work has a contribution to make, not only to the study of Soviet history, but to the development of approaches to the study of peasant societies in the world today.

In Part I below, an account is given by Terry Cox of the research of the Agrarian Marxists, of their critique of existing approaches to the study of peasant class differentiation, their theoretical and methodological innovations, and some of the details of their research approaches and their findings. This is followed in Part II by an analysis by Gary Littlejohn of state policy in relation to the Soviet rural class structure in the 1920s. This draws on the work of Kritsman and offers an interpretation of how it can be located in the context of the wider debates on the nature of the NEP period and the lessons to be drawn for policies of socialist construction. Part III is a condensed and edited translation by Gary Littlejohn of Kritsman's book, *The Class Stratification of the Soviet Countryside,* which is referred to above. This offers an interesting illustration of Kritsman's work and an insight into the complexity of the society he undertook to study.

NOTES

1. In contrast to many of the researchers working in the area of research on the Soviet countryside, Kritsman's background was not in the tradition of the zemstvo statistics or studies of peasant production but in the politics and theoretical debates of the revolutionary movement. Born in 1890, he joined the RSDLP in 1905, spent many years in exile abroad and finally returned to Russia in 1918, at which time he became a member of the Bolshevik Party. He held a series of posts in the V.S.N.Kh., became a member of the presidium of Gosplan, and published a number of works on aspects of economic planning and the Soviet national economy. He was a keen proponent, along with Larin and Milyutin on the idea of a 'single economic plan' for the Soviet economy (for which he attracted criticisms from Lenin), and in general, he was a supporter of the rapid development of a planned economy. With the introduction of the NEP, he argued unsuccessfully alongside Preobrazhenskii Trotsky and Larin against the weakening of the planning organisations.

   With the defeat of the policies he had supported, Kritsman moved away from administrative roles to become a leading academic figure, gaining membership in 1923, of the presidium of the Communist Academy. While at first maintaining some interest in planning, especially in relation to agriculture, his interests shifted more to the history of the revolution and to social analysis of the peasantry and agrarian questions. In 1925 his history of the War Communism period was published, and remains to this day probably the most thorough and authoritative history of the period [*Kritsman,* 1925b]. In 1924 Kritsman joined a special commission set up by the Communist Academy to study the history of the agrarian revolution in Russia. This was to be a vast enterprise, analysing in detail the statistics of change in various aspects of agriculture during the period of the revolution and into the 1920s. The first of several planned volumes was published under Kritsman's editorship in 1928 [*Kritsman,* 1928b], containing discussions of methodological issues associated with the research and a collection of some of the data used. Further volumes were promised but, with the political events of the 1930s overtaking the researchers, were never produced.

   During the 1920s, Kritsman also had other interests including membership of the editorial board of *Pravda,* editorships of the *Ekonomicheskaya Entsiklopediya* and of the journal *Problemy Ekonomiki,* and from 1927 membership of the Central Statistical Board. However, his major interest was to become the analysis of contemporary Soviet peasant agriculture. He became head of the Agrarian Section of the Communist Academy (later to become the Agrarian Institute), and the editor of the journal of the Agrarian Section, *Na Agrarnom Fronte*. From the mid-1920s he published a number of works on agrarian topics, some criticising prevailing ideas and methods of research and data collection on agriculture, some attacking the theories of the Organisation and Production School, and some, the major part of his work, attempting to develop a Marxist approach to the study of the peasantry and its class differentiation.

2. For further biographical information on members of the Agrarian Marxist School, see Solomon [1977: 189–191].

I. Class Analysis of the Russian Peasantry: The Research of Kritsman and his School

Terry Cox

One of the central issues in Russian Marxism's analysis of the peasantry was the question of its differentiation into the classes of capitalism. Such a development had been predicted by Plekhanov and evidence for it had been sought and provided by Lenin. However, after the Revolution of 1917 with its widespread redistribution of the land there grew up a strong current of opinion in Soviet ruling circles which tended to play down the question of renewed capitalist development in the countryside, and which, as a consequence, gave low priority to research on the differentiation of the peasantry.

Nevertheless, from about 1925 such questions again began to receive serious attention and, in the context, increasing disquiet was expressed about the usefulness of the kind of agrarian statistics being produced at the time. Various critiques of existing figures and research approaches were advanced, most notably by Kritsman [1926b and Part III below] and Yakovlev [1926]. Having shown in his work of 1926 how misleading the standard approaches could be, it fell to Kritsman to promote research and discussion of new methods of identifying the class characteristics of peasant households. The results of this initiative will be discussed below, after a brief outline of the Russian tradition of agrarian research and the critique of it which Kritsman and his colleagues developed.

1. RUSSIAN RESEARCH ON THE DIFFERENTIATION OF THE PEASANTRY BEFORE THE REVOLUTION

From the 1890s onwards there was much debate in Russia on the extent and significance of inequalities between peasant households. Views ranged from those of Lenin that the inequalities were signs of the gradual differentiation of classes of agrarian capitalists and proletarians, to those of Chayanov that the inequalities were mainly a reflection of demographic processes associated with the generational cycle of peasant households. In the former view capitalist development would lead gradually to the dissolution of the peasantry while in the latter view it would be compatible with the preservation and development of peasant agriculture [*Lenin*, 1899; *Chayanov*, 1925].

The usual criteria in these debates for deciding how peasant households should be grouped into different strata or classes were indicators of the size and well-being of farms (for example, area of land held in the household's allotment, area of land sown, number of head of working animals). During the first two decades of the 20th century sown area gradually replaced area of allotment as the preferred indicator for many parts of Russia, and was used both by Lenin [1899] and Chayanov [1915]. Sown area had the advantage of being easy to measure compared with more complex measurements of peasant wealth in a society with widespread illiteracy, and it was also generally thought to provide an accurate representation of differences in wealth between farms in many regions. In some parts of Russia, however, draught animals were preferred by local statisticians.

2. THE METHODOLOGICAL DEBATE IN THE 1920s

After the Revolution agrarian statistics were put on a firmer and more centrally organised basis by the Soviet government. In place of the separate *zemstvo* statistical bureaux there was now a Central Statistical Board (Ts.S.U.) as well as local government statistical officers. However, the leading figure in this new organisation who was concerned with data relating to the question of peasant differentiation was A. I. Khryashcheva who favoured collecting data on the basis of the indicators and methods which had become established in the years leading up to the Revolution. Under Khryashcheva's influence, Soviet agrarian statistics retained sown area as the main indicator of peasant wealth. In defending this she even suggested that it had become a more accurate indicator in the post-revolutionary period given the decline of sources of peasant income outside agriculture following the destruction of war and civil war [*Khryashcheva, 1926*].

The leading voice in opposition to this new orthodoxy was that of Kritsman. His dissatisfaction was initially provoked by a comparison of two sets of figures provided by the Ts.S.U. on the distribution of sown area and working animals among Russian peasant farms. While in the RSFSR between 1917 and 1920 the proportion of households not sowing grain fell from 15.9 per cent to 8.1 per cent, the proportion without working animals stayed constantly much higher at 27.0 per cent and 27.1 per cent respectively. Thus the proportion of farms sowing grain despite a complete lack of working animals rose from 11.1 per cent in 1917 to 19.0 per cent in 1920. To quote Kritsman:

> In other words, a number of those who managed farms did not have at their disposal the basic conditions for their management, working cattle, and consequently the number of farms engaged in agriculture wholly dependent on stronger farms rose, although at the same time the number of farms not engaged in their own cultivation fell [*Kritsman, 1925d, part 1: 50*].

Kritsman drew the conclusion that if an accurate picture of the emerging pattern of differentiation under NEP were to be drawn then new indicators would have to be adopted. He argued firstly that stratification by sown area was inadequate because the differentiation of the peasantry was taking place no longer on the basis of how much land was available for cultivation by a household but on the basis of the ownership of scarce working animals and farm stock. Levelling, in terms of the distribution of land which had taken place since the Revolution, masked the true extent of the growth of class differences.

Secondly, he argued that although stratification by ownership of animals and stock could show fairly accurately the extent of proletarianisation because at least it measured the distribution of the particular factor bringing about the dependence of weaker farms, nevertheless, it was not adequate as an overall indicator because it could not distinguish between farms with adequate distribution and farms with excess distribution of means of production which they could use to exploit weaker farms and begin to accumulate capital.

Basically there had always been a problem with stratification indices in that they were all indirect indicators of class relations. They did not directly measure relations involving the expropriation of the surplus of some peasant farms by others. Before the Revolution this had not seemed too great a problem since the indirect indicators were at least thought to provide an accurate reflection of class relations, but if this was no longer the case, a new approach had to be developed. Clearly the most direct indicator of capitalist class relations would be the hire and sale of labour power, but the problem with this was (and is) that it only becomes a prominent feature of capitalism once it has developed. In the very early stages of capitalist development within a petty-commodity economy the appropriation by some peasant households of the fruits of the labour of other households for capital accumulation would not necessarily be by such direct methods.

In the Russian countryside of the NEP period exploitative relations would to some extent occur in the traditional forms of a pre-capitalist society such as moneylending or the 'loan' of capital at varying rates of interest paid in kind or in labour services. The situation was further complicated by legal bans on the hire of labour and rent of land, especially in the early 1920s, which meant that peasants involved in such transactions would do their best to conceal them from researchers and taxmen alike. The result was that transactions took place in hidden (*skrytye*) forms such as in the guise of intra-familial exchanges or of amalgamations between farms. According to Kritsman, a widespread form of exploitation involved the hiring out of working animals and stock in such a way that the hidden capitalist appeared in the guise of a worker, working on another's farm with his own animals and stock, and a proletarian in the guise of an owner without working animals or stock hiring the owner of these necessary means of production. [*Kritsman,* 1925d, part 4: 42.] Despite superficial appearances, in this situation the peasant doing the manual labour was the exploiter because in return for his services as a ploughman providing his own horse and plough he received the greater share of the harvest sown and harvested by the 'owner' on the 'owner's' land.

> In these relationships the surplus value appropriated by the capitalist is not created by the labour of the hired 'worker' with his horse and stock, but by the labour of the hiring boss (*khozyain*); the labour of the latter

becomes possible only thanks to the fact that the means of production of
the hired man are employed on (the hirer's farm); whether (the hired
man) works with them or not does not alter the essence of the situation.
[Kritsman, 1925d, part 4: 42; Kritsman, 1926; see Part III below,
p. 85].

In other words, it was still labour which produced surplus value, but in this
transitional set of relationships, the phenomenal legal forms were completely
at odds with the true economic relationships. As in developed capitalism, it
was ownership of the means of production which provided a basis for their
owner to exploit the labour of another, but the situation was complex here
because different means of production were owned by different people.
Although land is usually thought to be the most important of the means of
production in agriculture, and the one whose ownership would provide the key
to the exploitation of the labour of the people who are hired to work on it,
Kritsman was suggesting that there was nothing inevitable about such a set of
circumstances. In the particular conditions of the NEP, it was, in varying
degrees, working animals and farm stock whose ownership offered the greater
economic power and enabled the owner of them to exploit the labour of others,
who, although they might own land, could not work it without hiring means of
production on terms which gave the owner of them the power over the surplus
value produced instead of the owner of the land. Thus, although both the owner
of the land and the owner of the horse and plough worked on the land, the
return to the latter, formally for his work in ploughing the land, would also
contain surplus value created by the labour of the landowner who worked for
the rest of the year.
   The facts that both 'owners' still worked on the land themselves, and that
ownership of the various means of production were split between them, was for
Kritsman, a reflection of the early stage of capitalist development then
prevalent in the Soviet countryside. He described the phenomena he was
analysing as 'incomplete capitalist forms'. Nevertheless, he was in no doubt
that the logic of the situation in abstract (if it were not for the context provided
by Soviet state power), would lead to full capitalist development, and that it
was therefore valid to interpret the forms of exploitation going on as already in
essence capitalist, despite their 'incompleteness'.
   The problem was that the existing Soviet agrarian statistics did not reveal
the tendencies which Kritsman saw emerging. He drew his own conclusions,
outlined above, from his extensive review of available local studies which is
translated in Part III below. However, although such literature provided
evidence of trends towards class differentiation occurring in hidden forms, its
data was still incomplete. Consequently, Kritsman and his colleagues
advocated a new approach based on the collection of data on direct class
indices such as the hire and sale of labour power, the rent and lease of land and
the hire and lease of stock and working animals. The aim was to use such data
to classify farms according to their dominant tendency in terms of potential
class relations. Although most farms would probably enter into a variety of

relations with other farms (including some where they exploited others, some where they were exploited by others, and possibly even some involving genuine co-operation), Kritsman reasoned that it should be possible to discover the predominant balance of relations engaged in by a particular farm and use this to characterise the class nature of that farm.

3. THE RESEARCH OF V. S. NEMCHINOV

Following Kritsman's critical review of existing agrarian statistics (Part III below) a number of attempts were made to devise and test slightly different schemes for the measurement of the extent of the above-mentioned tendencies. The first such attempt was made by V. S. Nemchinov, a statistician working in the Urals region, and not a member of the Moscow-based Kritsman group. (Nemchinov was later to become a leading economist in the Krushchev period.) Under the influence of Kritsman's initial work, Nemchinov developed an approach taking four basic factors of production as his indicators and cross-classifying these according to who owned them and whether they were used for farming on the peasant's own farm or that of another peasant. A farm whose relations were predominantly expropriating was termed 'entrepreneurial', while a farm whose relations were predominantly exploited was termed 'dependent'. A farm whose relations were more or less in balance between exploiting and exploited tendencies was considered to be an 'independent' farm. The scheme could be presented according to the table below:

TABLE 1

CONDITIONS AND MEANS OF PRODUCTION IN PEASANT AGRICULTURE

	Means of production on own farm:		Own means of production:
	others	own	on others farm
land	entrepreneurial	independent	dependent
basic capital (cattle stock, farm buildings)	dependent	independent	entrepreneurial
variable capital (seed, fodder, fertiliser)	dependent	independent	entrepreneurial
labour power	entrepreneurial	independent	dependent

[*Nemchinov*, 1926b: 48]

The extent of entrepreneurship, dependence or independence could be calculated by ascertaining the monetary value, or working out a monetary equivalent for the factors involved in each transaction. From the results obtained the farms could be grouped into categories relative to their overall predominant tendencies. Nemchinov used the following groupings:

1. Dependent   a) More than 50 per cent dependent in their relations with other farms;
                     b) 15–50 per cent dependent;
2. Independent   a) 2.5–15 per cent dependent;
                     b) up to 2.5 per cent dependent or up to 2.5 per cent entrepreneurial;
                     c) 2.5–15 per cent entrepreneurial;
3. Entrepreneurial – More than 15 per cent entrepreneurial.

Thus, echoing Kritsman, the most important factors in determining a household's class position were the means of production in animals and farm stock. An adequate or surplus supply of them assured a position of strength. Overcapacity in these means of production enabled a farm to either rent extra land and hire extra labour in order to use them more fully, or to lease them out at such advantageous rates, that as Kritsman had noted, the transaction was in fact a hidden form of acquiring extra land. In contrast, undercapacity would require a farm to enter into relations where its inability to farm without essential means of production would be seriously exploited. On the other hand, undercapacity in other factors, such as land or labour, could be resolved more easily since, compared with draught animals or ploughs, these were more easily available.[1]

The whole procedure of using the criteria of 'own' or 'other's' means of production and labour on 'own' or 'other's' farm as indicators of the class character of farms was of course a necessarily roundabout way of uncovering class relations. Ideally, the best way would have been to acquire direct information about actual transactions between farms, discovering exactly how much was paid for each hour of labour, for each unit of hire of means of production, and each unit of land rented, and compare this with the value of the surplus produced. However, since only developed capitalist enterprises would carry out the kind of detailed accounting that would make such data available, information could only be gathered by the more indirect approach described above.

Having established the likely meaning of the various possible transactions in factors of production for the specific circumstances under study, the next step was to fix the value of each factor in order to be able to weigh various relations against each other and establish the overall balance on each farm of elements of entrepreneurial, dependent and independent farming. Such calculations could only be made, Nemchinov argued, either by ascertaining the prevailing local monetary value, or working out money equivalents for each factor involved in the transactions. Again, since accurate information on exact amounts involved could not be discovered, it had to be assumed that most transactions were conducted at the standard rate for the given time and place.

Using information collected by local statisticians, including much that had been collected in the dynamic census for Troitskii *okrug* in the Urals, Nemchinov was able to establish prevailing local rates and prices for the area of his study [*Nemchinov,* 1926b: 53–5]. It was then possible to put values to the transactions of all the farms in the sample and, according to the formula shown in Table I above, establish the overall class character of each farm. Examples of the figures for two farms in Troitskii *okrug* are shown below in Table 2.

TABLE 2

EVALUATION OF FARMS
(in roubles)

	Factors of production on own farm				Peasant's own means of production on someone else's farm		TOTALS
	belonging to someone else		belonging to own farm				
a) *Farm N.A. G-dov*							
arable land & hay fields	(e)	27.25	(i)	76.84	(d)	—	104.09
stock and animals	(d)	—	(i)	104.58	(e)	11.0	115.58
seed and fodder	(d)	—	(i)	499.66	(e)	—	499.66
labour power	(e)	351.00	(i)	365.00	(d)	—	716.00
TOTALS		378.25		1046.08		11.0	1435.33
b) *Farm N.P.B-noi*							
arable land & hay fields	(e)	—	(i)	23.88	(d)	17.99	41.87
stock and animals	(d)	20.99	(i)	0.38	(e)	—	21.37
seed and fodder	(d)	8.24	(i)	10.29	(e)	—	18.53
labour power	(e)	—	(i)	213.33	(d)	266.67	480.00
TOTAL		29.23		247.88		284.66	561.77

(e) = entrepreneurial   (d) = dependent   (i) = independent
[*Nemchinov,* 1926b: 55]

The sum of entrepreneurial elements in farm (a) was (27.25 + 351.00 + 11.0 =)R389.25, while the sum of the independent elements was R1046.08, there being no dependent elements. In the absence of any dependent elements, the overall character of the farm could then be established simply by calculating the extent of entrepreneurial activity as a percentage of the total value of the household's own means of production employed on their own farm. For farm (a) this worked out at 37.2 per cent entrepreneurial.

In farm (b) on the other hand, there were dependent and independent, but no entrepreneurial elements. The sum of dependent elements was (20.99 + 8.24 +17.99 + 266.67 =)R313.89 while the value of independent elements was R247.88. In the absence of entrepreneurial elements, the overall character of farm (b) could then be established by calculating the dependent elements as a percentage of the independent elements, giving a result of 126.63 per cent dependent [*Nemchinov*, 1926b: 55–6].

Other farms might be more complex, with elements of both entrepreneurship and dependence in their operations. In such cases the value of each as a percentage of independent elements had to be calculated and the balance taken in order to find the overall characteristic tendency of the farm.

In their research, Nemchinov and his team carried out such evaluations of 835 farms in the steppe area of Troitskii *okrug* (taking for the sake of simplicity only those which had not experienced any 'organic changes' such as division or merger). They found the following distribution of types in their sample:

TABLE 3

DISTRIBUTION OF FARMS BY CLASS CHARACTERISTICS IN TROITSKII *OKRUG*

Type of farm	Numbers	Percentage
More than 50% dependent	81	9.7
15%–50% dependent	109	13.1
2.5%–15% dependent	81	9.7
2.5% dependent to 2.5% entrepreneurial	442	52.9
2.5% to 15% entrepreneurial	101	12.1
15% to 30% entrepreneurial	15	1.8
More than 30% entrepreneurial	6	0.7
TOTAL	835	100

[*Nemchinov*, 1926b: 57]

Having arrived at this grouping of farms, Nemchinov then sought to compare it with more conventional approaches using so-called 'natural indicators' such as sown area and ownership of animals.

As can be seen from Table 4, the different groupings produced very different patterns of distribution. For Nemchinov this helped to confirm further the arguments against the use of 'natural indicator' groupings for the study of peasant class relations. For example, the bottom groups in terms of sown area and ownership of animals were all well represented not only in the dependent farm groups but also among the independent farms, including small numbers which even displayed slightly entrepreneurial tendencies. At the other end of the scale, some farms in the top groups by natural indicators appeared in the independent rather than the entrepreneurial groups.

However, although Nemchinov held to his claims for the superiority of his approach in revealing the patterns of class relations within the peasantry, he seems not to have regarded such an approach as completely sufficient by itself. In order to identify actual groups in terms of their class position, he proposed to combine the above grouping with one based on annual expenditure on constant capital per farm. Such a measure, for Nemchinov, not only gave a more accurate indication of the level of well-being of a farm, but also showed its relative economic strength in precisely those factors which would affect its

TABLE 4

COMPARISON OF GROUPINGS BY DIFFERENT INDICATORS

| | Grouping by dependent and entrepreneurial elements | | | | | | | |
| | dependent farms | | independent farms | | | entrepreneurial | | Totals |
Grouping by natural indicators	more than 50%	15–50%	15–2.5% dep.	2.5% entr. 2.5% dep.	2.5–15% entr.	15–30%	more than 30%	
All farms	81	109	81	442	101	15	6	835
A. Sown area (in *desyatin*)								
Not sowing	24	6	3	15	—	—	—	48
0.1–2	45	52	28	63	2	—	—	190
2.1–4	6	47	33	117	5	—	1	209
4.1–6	6	3	10	104	6	1	1	131
6.1–10	—	1	6	94	30	6	1	138
10.1–16	—	—	1	37	35	7	—	80
16.1–25	—	—	—	10	14	1	3	28
More than 25	—	—	—	2	9	—	—	11
B. Working animals								
None	71	61	25	59	—	—	—	216
1	9	44	41	171	10	1	—	276
2	1	4	12	118	14	9	3	161
3	—	—	2	55	24	2	2	85
4–7	—	—	1	39	53	3	1	97
C. Cows								
None	44	17	8	26	—	—	—	95
1	30	68	44	135	3	2	1	283
2	5	21	21	143	28	2	3	223
3	2	3	2	87	18	5	—	117
4 and more	—	—	6	51	52	6	2	117

[*Nemchinov*, 1926b: 57]

potential for either entrepreneurship or dependence. Expenditure on constant capital, which included all expenditure on materials in production except labour power would be a measure of a farm's provision in those factors which, as Nemchinov had already argued, were the basis for the most significant relations of exploitation in the Soviet countryside.

Although there was no close correspondence between the results of the two groupings, there was a clear tendency for the more entrepreneurial farms to spend more on constant capital, and to have a higher organic composition of capital, as can be seen from the tables below.

TABLE 5

EXPENDITURE ON CONSTANT CAPITAL BY DIFFERENT CLASS GROUPS

Entrepreneurial and dependent elements	Annual expenditure on constant capital per farm (in roubles)				
	poor		middle		well-to-do
	up to 100	100–200	200–500	500–700	More than 700
More than 50% dep.	67	9	5	—	—
15–50% dependent	36	53	20	—	—
2.5–15% dependent	16	34	27	3	1
2.5% dep.–2.5% entr.	40	88	233	49	32
2.5–15% entr.	—	3	18	29	51
More than 15% entr.	—	—	7	6	8
Totals	159	187	310	87	92

[*Nemchinov*, 1926b: 61]

TABLE 6

ORGANIC COMPOSITION OF CAPITAL IN DIFFERENT CLASS GROUPS

Grouping by social character	% of farms where for 1 rouble of labour power there was constant capital to the value of (in kopeks)					
	up to 10	11–20	21–30	31–50	51–100	more than 100
More than 50% dependent	33.33	28.40	19.75	12.35	6.17	—
15–50% dep.	4.59	15.60	15.60	37.61	28.85	2.75
2.5–15% dep.	1.23	11.11	9.88	37.04	30.87	9.87
2.5% dep. –2.5% entr.	1.36	1.58	4.75	18.33	40.72	33.26
2.5–15% entr.	—	—	—	0.99	22.77	76.24
More than 15% entrepreneurial	—	—	—	—	23.81	76.19

[*Nemchinov*, 1926b: 60]

The implication here in Nemchinov's thinking was that, although a few relatively poor and middle farms were entrepreneurial in their relations with others, they would be less likely than their economically stronger entrepreneurial neighbours to be able to continually strengthen their position and become fully capitalist farms. The most likely candidates for full membership of an emerging class of capitalist farmers would be those able to spend more on scarce means of production, giving themselves a higher organic composition of capital, obliging them to seek to employ the labour of other households in order to fully utilise their capital, and thus to extract surplus value from the labour of their neighbours. Thus, as a result of combining the two groupings, Nemchinov felt able to delineate class membership in his sample. From the evidence of Table 5, there were 8 clearly *kulak* (capitalist) farms, or 0.96 per cent of the sample. These were the farms that were both more than 15 per cent entrepreneurial and classified as well off. On the other hand, there were 165 proletarian farms (20 per cent of the sample) who were more than 15 per cent dependent and classified as poor. The rest of the sample could be classified as either poor, middle or well-to-do independent producers [*Nemchinov,* 1926b: 58–61].[2]

In his Urals research, Nemchinov had thus provided a trial run for a method of applying Kritsman's ideas in empirical research. His method attempted not only the examination of the extent of the relations through which, it was suggested, class formation was taking place, but also, through his combination of two groupings, the delineation of class groups and therefore of the emerging class structure of the peasantry.

In his conclusion, Nemchinov turned to the further use of his approach. He thought it would be impracticable to fully analyse the data of all agrarian censuses using his scheme, and suggested that samples of no more than 10 per cent or even 5 per cent would be adequate to encompass the range of variation in any given area. In this way Nemchinov advocated the adoption of his approach nationally by the Ts.S.U. so that a nationwide class analysis of the Soviet countryside would become possible as part of the annual data collection for the dynamic censuses. Over time, this would then reveal the changing class structure of the Soviet countryside as a commodity economy became established [*Nemchinov,* 1926b: 61–2].

4. KRITSMAN'S RESPONSE TO NEMCHINOV'S RESEARCH

Nemchinov's work marked a significant advance in the development of empirical research on the class structure of the peasantry. Kritsman greeted its publication with great enthusiasm and saw it as confirming the approach he had been developing in his 1925 articles. In particular, 'it confirms above all that capitalist farming on the basis of the hiring out of means of production is the *basic* form of capitalist farming in the Soviet countryside' [*Kritsman* 1926–7, part 1–4]. Furthermore, Nemchinov provided important support in the argument against the views of the Organisation and Production School that the peasant farm could be seen as a self-sufficient independent unit producing for its own needs from its own resources. Nemchinov had not only helped show that transactions between farms were a vital part of peasant agricultural production, but that they could be accounted for in research and built into a research approach aimed at discovering the class structure of the peasantry.

However, Kritsman also suggested some criticisms and modifications of Nemchinov's scheme which were to be important in further empirical research which was to follow. Kritsman's basic criticism concerned Nemchinov's understanding of the terms 'dependence', 'independence' and 'entrepreneurship' which he described as 'slip-shod'. Nemchinov had assumed that for each of his four categories of factors of production, a sufficient definition of independent use of them was that they were owned by a peasant household and

used on the farm of that household. However, while this worked well enough
for both Nemchinov's categories of basic and circulating capital, it worked less
well for either labour power or land.

As noted above, both Kritsman and Nemchinov had argued that agrarian
capitalism was developing primarily out of the relations concerned with the
hire and lease of means of production and that surplus value was appropriated
not simply through the hire of labour power, but through the hire of labour
power mediated through the hire and lease of the more scarce, and therefore in
this context more basic, factors of working animals and farm stock.
Nemchinov had accepted this as a general proposition but, Kritsman thought,
had not fully incorporated it into the logic of his approach.

This could be seen from Nemchinov's treatment of labour power and land in
his scheme, where he regarded them as separate factors to be treated in the
same way as, and on a par with, basic and circulating capital. For Kritsman,
labour power and land could not be considered independently of the access to
scarce means of production which allowed or denied their productive use. For
Kritsman, Nemchinov was wrong, therefore, to treat labour power, for
example, if it was a household's own labour power on its own farm, as
independent. It was necessary to ask a further question about whose means of
production made possible the household's cultivation of its own land. To the
extent that it was the peasant's own means of production which was used, then
his labour power could be considered an element of independent farming. If,
however, the means of production used on the farm were hired from someone
else, then surplus value would have been appropriated by their owner from the
labour of the household which had hired them and therefore that household's
labour should have been regarded as an element of dependence in the farm's
production organisation. Similarly, in relation to land, it could only be
classified among elements of independence if the household which owned it
also cultivated it with its own labour and own means of production. It was a
mistake, therefore, Kritsman argued, to view labour power, land and means of
production separately from one another as Nemchinov had done. It should
have been borne in mind that each was an element in the same transaction
involving other factors of production.

Following on from this criticism, Kritsman suggested a different approach
to the question:

> In place of these unclear relations of 'dependence' and 'entrepreneur-
> ship' it is necessary to put another with a more definite economic
> content, namely the relation of the means of production to labour power.
> This relation distinctively characterises every farm looked at from a
> social-class point of view.

There were three 'pure forms' of such relations between the means of
production and labour power:

1. A household's own means of production in conjunction only with its
   own labour power, and its own labour power in conjunction only with

its own means of production. This relationship was typical of a 'petit-bourgeois' farm.

2. A household's own means of production not used in conjunction with its own labour power, and only used in conjunction with the labour power of other households. This was typical of a 'capitalist' farm.

3. A household's own labour power not used in conjunction with its own means of production but only in conjunction with the means of production of others. This was typical of a 'proletarian' farm. There would, of course, also be intermediate types between the above pure types, made up of various combinations of the pure types.

[*Kritsman,* 1926–7, part 1: 8–9.]

Furthermore, in making his modifications of Nemchinov's approach, Kritsman also suggested discarding the terminology of 'dependence', 'independence' and 'entrepreneurship', and replacing them by terms which more directly reflected the class tendencies he saw inherent in the situation, that is, 'capitalist', 'petit-bourgeois' and 'proletarian'. Kritsman did not make his reasons for these changes clear, but they obviously reflected Kritsman's commitment to the view that the relations of exploitation revealed by Nemchinov's approach would result in the formation of distinct classes in the Soviet countryside if the tendencies were not arrested in time.

With the above criticisms in mind, Kritsman also suggested revisions in Nemchinov's method of calculating the degrees of dependence (proletarianisation), independence (petit-bourgeois farming) and entrepreneurship (capitalist development) within the peasantry. As noted above, Nemchinov had worked out the values separately of a series of different factors, each with its different meaning in terms of the class character of a farm, and had then added the values of each factor of each type to arrive at the relation between different tendencies. Kritsman, however, proposed to go more directly to the interrelations between aspects of a farm's operations in his method of calculation.

For farms of a proletarian or semi-proletarian type (that is, for farms which had high values of dependent elements according to Nemchinov's scheme), the relation of the household's own labour power used on its own farm to the sum of all its labour power should be calculated. Then, the relation of the value of its own means of production used on its own farm to the total value of all means of production used on its own farm should be calculated. The two figures obtained should then be multiplied to obtain the proportion of the household's own labour power used with its own means of production.

For farms of a capitalist or semi-capitalist type (exhibiting a high value of entrepreneurial elements according to Nemchinov's scheme), the relation of the household's own labour power to all labour power employed on the farm should be calculated. Then, the relation of the household's own means of production used on its farm to all means of production belonging to the household should be calculated. The two figures obtained should then be multiplied to obtain the proportion of the household's own means of production used by its own labour power [*Kritsman, 1926–7,* part 1: 10].

Kritsman illustrated this method of calculation using as his examples the same two farms used above to illustrate Nemchinov's scheme (Table 2). For farm (a), which Nemchinov had calculated as 37.2 per cent entrepreneurial, Kritsman argued as follows: (i) of all the labour power employed on it, R365.00 worth belonged to that household while R351.00 worth was the labour power of other peasants. In other words, the household's own labour power constituted 51.0 per cent of all the labour employed on its farm. (ii) The total value of the means of production used on this farm was R604.24, all of which belonged to the household. A further R11.00 belonging to the household was employed outside its own farm. In other words, 98.2 per cent of the household's own means of production was used on its own farm. (iii) From the above figures it followed that the household's own labour was only employed on 51.0 per cent of 98.2 per cent; that is, 50.1 per cent of the household's means of production.

The meaning of this for Kritsman was that the independent elements of the farm, where its own labour power was used in conjunction with its own means of production, amounted to 50.1 per cent, and therefore elements of entrepreneurship amounted to 49.9 per cent representing the proportion of the household's means of production employed through the exploitation of outside labour power. Thus, as opposed to Nemchinov's figure of 37.2 per cent entrepreneurial, Kritsman's scheme produced the figure of 49.9 per cent.

For farm (b), which Nemchinov had found to be 126.63 per cent dependent, Kritsman argued as follows: (i) all labour power employed on the farm belonged to the owning household, to the value of R213.37, and in addition, R266.67 of the household's labour power was employed outside its own farm. In other words, 44.4 per cent of the household's own labour was employed on its own farm. (ii) The household used all of its own means of production on its own farm, to the value of R10.67 and R29.23 worth of means of production belonging to others. In other words the household's own means of production used on its own farm amounted to 26.7 per cent of the total value of means of production used on it. (iii) Therefore, although 44.4 per cent of the household's labour power was employed on its own farm, only 26.7 per cent of this 44.4 per cent was used in conjunction with its own means of production. That is, 11.9 per cent of the farm's operation represented elements of independence.

It followed therefore that the remaining 88.1 per cent of the household's labour power was exploited through employment in conjunction with means of production belonging to others so that the farm was 88.1 per cent proletarian as opposed to Nemchinov's figure of 126.63 per cent dependent [*Kritsman, 1926–7,* part 1: 9–10].

Whereas Nemchinov had calculated entrepreneurship and dependence as proportions of the independent elements of a farm, thus allowing a result embodying the rather awkward concept of a farm being more than 100 per cent dependent, Kritsman calculated capitalist and proletarian elements as proportions of all the elements of a farm so that his figures were true percentages.[3]

Of course, the above examples, used for illustration, represented relatively straightforward farms in terms of their class character: that is either a mixture of capitalist/entrepreneurial and petit-bourgeois/independent or of proletarian/dependent and petit-bourgeois/independent. In reality, however, many farms might have contained all three elements. In such cases, Kritsman suggested, it would be necessary in making calculations to take the difference between contradictory elements. For example, if a household both sold its own labour power and hired labour to work on its own farm, the difference between the two values would be taken and this figure, representing either the extent to which capitalist elements predominated over proletarian elements or vice versa, would be used in the calculations as described above.

Kritsman's modifications had two main advantages over Nemchinov's original scheme. First, Kritsman's approach was able to separate the different class components more accurately, in particular providing a more satisfactory means of identifying elements of independent production. Secondly, his method of working gave a more straightforward and plausible presentation of the class character of farms, representing the relative strengths as percentages of a total of 100 per cent.

In making his modifications, however, Kritsman omitted one factor which had been part of Nemchinov's scheme without really discussing why he had done so. In his initial criticisms of Nemchinov, Kritsman argued that a household's own labour power and its own land could not necessarily be assumed to represent elements of independence in a farm's operations because their character would depend on whether they were used in conjunction with the household's own means of production. In his detailed modification, however, Kritsman dealt only with the different relations between labour power and means of production, but did not carry out a similar discussion for land. Obviously, labour power was of much greater significance for a discussion of class relations given its role as the source of value in Marxist theory, and it was particularly more significant than land in the conditions of the NEP where land had been redistributed and could no longer be bought and sold. Nevertheless, since land still had a rental value, it should, perhaps, have still been of sufficient importance to be taken into account. It seems likely, however, that including land in the calculations would not have made a great difference to the results obtained.

Kritsman's views on the relative importance of different factors for the overall class character of farms were reflected in his definition of peasant agriculture:

> Peasant farming is the farming of petty producers. A characteristic of them is the presence in their enterprise of their own means of production and its use by their own labour power. In other words . . . . the relation between its own labour power and its own means of production alone can characterise a peasant farm. . . . My grouping is

constructed and based on the calculation of this relation [*Kritsman,* 1926–7, part 2: 3].

Independent peasant farming in its ideal-typical form would be based on a correspondence between labour power and the means of production on the household's farm. To the extent that existing farms were moving away from independent farming, they would increasingly reveal a lack of correspondence between their own labour power and means of production. In the face of this lack of correspondence in a petty commodity economy, peasant farms were increasingly obliged either to turn their means of production into capital or to see their labour power alienated as a commodity.

In essence, therefore, Kritsman's approach involved the juxtaposition of six elements: own farm, other's farm, own means of production, other's means of production, own labour power and other's labour power. It was impossible, Kritsman warned, to construct any general theory about how these six elements were interrelated. This was something to be specified in relation to the object of study by empirical investigation. His proposed research approach would do this: (a) by specifying what interrelations of the six elements were to be found in peasant farms in order to identify qualitative or typological categories of farms; and (b) by calculating the extent in value terms to which different farms consisted of different combinations of the six elements. Farms would not necessarily be made up of simple combinations of elements. Many would comprise complex and contradictory combinations with different connotations for class membership. It was for this reason that Kritsman agreed with Nemchinov that a quantitative aspect of the grouping was also required in order to discover which class characteristics were predominant within the whole contradictory complex relations of any given farm [*Kritsman,* 1926–7, part 2: 5, 13].

On this basis Kritsman and others went on to develop empirical research on the nature of class relations within the Russian peasantry. Most of the surveys carried out by the Kritsman group were based on a combination of simple household survey and an adapted form of the more complex peasant budget survey methods which had been developed by Chayanov and other members of the Organisation and Production School, some of them using double-entry book-keeping to plot the various processes and transactions involved in the organisation of peasant farms. The results obtained were then used to classify farms according to which kinds of relations were predominant in their operations; that is, into exploiting (developing towards capitalist), independent and exploited (developing towards proletarian) peasant farms.

5. THE VOLOKOLAMSK RESEARCH

The next study to apply Kritsman's ideas was carried out by Anisimov, Vermenichev and Naumov in the flax-growing region of Volokolamsk near Moscow [1927]. This was also the first study to use the budget survey method for a study of peasant class relations. (The authors were particularly well placed to do this since they were research students under Chayanov in the early 1920s.) Their approach was to record the monetary value of their sample farms' transactions (or to estimate the value on the basis of local seasonally adjusted rates and prices where monetary exchange did not occur), and using double-entry accounting, to assess the nature of the various processes and transactions involved in the organisation of the peasant farms. The results obtained were then used to classify farms according to which kind of relations were found to be predominant in their operations; that is, into exploiting (developing towards capitalist) or exploited (becoming proletarian) peasant farms.

Having produced detailed accounts of their sample of peasant farms, the researchers assembled the following data:

1. *The value of all means of production belonging to a household.* This included both fixed and circulating capital used both in agriculture and in other production such as crafts. This value was represented by 'a'.
2. *The value of the household's own means of production leased out to other households.* This was represented by 'b'.
3. *The value of others' means of production employed on a household's own farm.* This included both animals and farm stock which had been hired by the household and circulating capital such as seed or cash which had been borrowed by the household. This was represented by 'c'.
4. *The value of all the labour power of a household,* including labour provided by its own members for its own agricultural, craft or trading activities, as well as labour hired and sold by it. This was represented by 'd'.
5. *The value of the household's own labour power employed in its own farm or other activities.* This was represented by 'e'.
6. *The value of the labour power hired by a household from outside* for work on its own farm or other activities. This was represented by 'f'.
7. *The value of the labour power sold by a household to others.* This was represented by 'g'.

Having established the above values for any given farm, the extent of independent production relative to either proletarian or capitalist tendencies could then be calculated using the following method derived from Kritsman.

First, for households selling their own labour or hiring stock (as well as for households with a more complex mixture of production relations where the value of the sale of labour power and hire of stock exceeded the value of the hire of workers and leasing out of stock), the relation of the value of the household's own means of production used in its own production to all means of production used by it was represented by 'xp' where

$$xp = \frac{a - c}{a} \quad \text{or} \quad \frac{a - (c - b)}{a}$$

Secondly, for the same type of households, the relation of their own labour power used on their own farm to all of their labour was represented by 'yp' where

$$yp = \frac{e}{d} \quad \text{or} \quad \frac{e}{e+(g-f)}$$

The ratio of independent elements to proletarian elements was then worked out by multiplying xp by yp and multiplying the result by 100. This gave the extent of independent elements expressed as a percentage of all activities of the household. The degree of proletarianisation as a percentage of the total was then obtained simply by subtracting the figure for independent elements from 100.

A similar method was used in respect of households with capitalist tendencies. For those households leasing out stock or hiring labour (or where the extent of these relations was greater than the extent of hiring stock and selling labour power), the relation of the household's own means of production used on its own farm or other business to all of its means of production was represented by 'xk' where

$$xk = \frac{a}{a+b} \quad \text{or} \quad \frac{a}{a+(b-c)}$$

The relation of the household's own labour power used on its own farm or business to all labour power used by it was represented by 'yk' where

$$yk = \frac{e}{d} \quad \text{or} \quad \frac{e}{e+(f-g)}$$

By multiplying xk and yk and multiplying the result by 100, the percentage of independent elements was found, and if this figure was subtracted from 100, the percentage of capitalist elements was obtained [*Anisimov et al.*, 1927: 37–8].

By pioneering their new use of budget research, Anisimov and his colleagues believed they had actually provided enough details on the production relations of farms finally to fulfil demands made by Kritsman and Nemchinov for a grouping which synthesised qualitative indicators, and directly to measure tendencies of class formation. On the basis of their results, they suggested that the Volokolamsk peasantry should be divided into five groups representing various tendencies and degrees of class formation, as follows:

    I Proletarian households with a small plot of land.
    II Semi-proletarian households, farming but with elements of proletarianisation.
    III Small commodity producing households which could develop in either class direction.

IV Semi-capitalist households with rudiments of capitalist farming, evolving on a capitalist path.

V Capitalist, predominantly small capitalist, households.

[*Anisimov et al.,* 1927: 33–4]

The problem was, however, that although the research produced much evidence on relations of exploitation between households, and although it was able to measure the extent to which households were exploiting, exploited or independent, the exact boundaries of different groups within the peasantry remained difficult to work out. Given that they were dealing with a continuing process (which they saw as one of class formation) it would always be somewhat arbitrary for the researchers to draw clear boundaries at any particular point between households. Thus, even after the impressive methodological advances in their research, there still remained a final stage which involved exercising intuition concerning, for example, exactly what percentage of capitalist tendencies constituted a small capitalist, as opposed to a semi-capitalist household, or where to draw the line between proletarian and semi-proletarian, or, even more difficult, what range of percentage points of either value sign should constitute the middle group of small commodity producers. In the sample there were no cases where a household was 100 per cent capitalist, proletarian or independent. They were all more complex hybrids, involving elements of at least independent farming with either capitalist or proletarian tendencies, and in some cases, with mixtures of all three characteristics.

The solution decided upon by the research team, no doubt under the influence of Nemchinov's earlier research, but with distinct differences in their chosen boundaries, was as follows:

TABLE 7

DISTRIBUTION OF FARMS BY CLASS CHARACTERISTICS

	Type	Number of households in sample
I	50.1% and more proletarian	5
II	20.1%–50% proletarian	6
III	0–20% proletarian	21
IV	0–20% capitalist	22
V	20.1% and more capitalist	6

[*Anisimov et al.,* 1927: 39]

In order to provide support for the grouping of their sample in this way, Anisimov and his colleagues provided the following table showing the differences between their chosen groups according to the various criteria shown.

The presentation of data in Table 8 helped confirm the validity of the research and its grouping of households in a number of ways. First, it could be shown that the most proletarianised households were also the poorest groups

TABLE 8

VALUE (IN ROUBLES) OF MEANS OF PRODUCTION AND LABOUR
POWER ON AVERAGE PER HOUSEHOLD PER GROUP

GROUPS

	I	II	III	IV	V
Total value of all means of production in the budget year	245.63	532.74	652.57	1003.17	1635.07
Value of own means of production on own farm	190.95	459.14	626.57	953.59	1547.50
Value of other's means of production on own farm	54.68	73.60	26.0	—	—
Value of own means of production on other's farm	—	—	—	49.54	87.57
Total value of labour power in the budget year	567.59	462.11	630.81	835.01	1818.41
Value of own labour power on own farm	253.11	375.53	615.81	826.46	1398.55
Value of hired labour on own farm	—	—	—	26.55	419.86
Value of own labour power sold	314.58	86.58	15.06	—	—

[*Anisimov et al.,* 1927: 39]

in terms of the total value of means of production, and that their own means of production on their own farm was the lowest for any group. Linking this to the fact that the value of their labour power on their own farm was also the lowest for any group, it was clear that they had insufficient means of production to employ their own labour power effectively on their own farm.[4] It could also be seen that the relative well-being of farms on all these counts improved progressively from the most proletarian through to the most capitalist group.

Secondly it could be shown that there was a clear divide between the capitalist-oriented groups who bought labour power and leased out means of production, and the proletarian-oriented groups (including group III) who all sold labour power and hired means of production. It seems that the grouping was so accurately delineated that no farms in the capitalist-oriented groups IV and V hired any stock or sold any labour power, and no farms in the proletarian-oriented groups I, II and III leased out any stock or hired any labour. Furthermore, in the case of labour power, the more capitalist the group the more labour power it bought, while the more proletarian the group the more labour power it sold. In relation to means of production, the situation was slightly more complicated in that while the more capitalist the farm the more it leased out stock, and while the marginally proletarian group III hired less stock than the more proletarian group II, the most proletarian group I also hired less stock than group II. Although the research team did not discuss this, it can probably be explained by the tendency of group I households to live mainly by wage-labour with only a subsidiary plot so that they would not have been strongly motivated to hire much stock.

Overall, the researchers felt able to conclude that the figures showed 'our method of grouping more or less reveals the socio-economic types of farm' [*Anisimov et al.*, 1927: 41]. In that the research did give a clear picture of the production relations of peasant farming and a grouping of households which corresponded with the data on such relations, their claim was quite justified and their research was received with great interest by their colleagues. However, it also met with some criticism (which will be discussed below) and some disappointment in that Anisimov and his group never went on to produce a detailed analysis of the characteristics of peasant farms in each of the class groups they had identified. In this, their work was less interesting than some of the later studies by the Agrarian Marxists which were in fact based on less-sophisticated data than the Volokolamsk study.

6. THE SAMARA RESEARCH

Further studies followed the basic research approach adopted in the Volokolamsk study, but each also contributed methodological innovations of its own. For example, the next survey, carried out by Vermenichev, Gaister and Raevich in Samara *guberniya* tried out a simpler system of measurement of the various inter-household relations under study.

To begin with, the approach adopted by the researchers was to examine each kind of relationship separately to find out the best way in practice of measuring it, and then after that, to find a way of expressing all the different measurements on a common scale. Each relation was therefore measured in terms of different indicators. The hire and sale of labour power was measured in numbers of days of the duration of the transaction; lease of stock and animals was measured in terms of the cash (or cash-equivalent) income received from it; hire of stock and animals in terms of the numbers and kinds of items hired; the rent of land in *desyatins* rented; and the leasing out of land in terms of the proportion of leased land to the total land of the farm.

In order to bring together the profusion of measurements, a common scale was chosen based on a system of allocating points. Varying numbers of points were allocated according to the degree of exploitation, measured on a scale of positive numbers, or the degree of dependence, measured on a scale of negative numbers. The translation of the different measurements on to the points scale was carried out as follows.

Hire of labour power		*Sale of labour power*	
Up to 10 days per annum	+1	Up to 10 days p.a.	−1
11–50 days p.a.	+3	11–30 days p.a.	−3
51–90 days p.a.	+4	31–50 days p.a.	−4
More than 90 days p.a.	+5	More than 50 days p.a.	−5

Leasing out cattle or stock		*Hire of cattle or stock*	
Income of up to 10 roubles	+1	Hiring simple stock only, or no more than 2 items of advanced equipment	−1
Income of up to 11–50R	+2	Hiring working cattle and 3 or more	
Income of more than 50R	+3	items of advanced equipment	−2
Rent of Land		*Leasing out of land*	
Up to 2 *desyatins*	+1	Up to 30% of own arable land	−1
More than 2 *desyatins*	+2	More than 30% of own arable land	−2

[*Vermenichev et al.*, 1928: 43]

The overall balance of the points score of each household was then used to classify households into groups according to their overall class characteristics. A five group classification was used along the lines indicated below:

	Class group	*Points*
I	The agricultural proletariat living mainly by the sale of their labour power.	−5 or less
II	Small producers with signs of dependence on others, managing to farm only by also selling some labour power or by hiring working cattle or farm stock.	from −4 to −2
III	Independent or neutral small producers mainly with their own labour power and with only limited involvement in hiring or selling labour, or renting or leasing stock.	from −1 to +1
IV	Small producers with some entrepreneurial activity, hiring some wage labour or leasing out some stock.	from +2 to +4
V	Semi-capitalist or small capitalist farmers, farming by means of large amounts of wage labour.	+5 or more

[*Vermenichev et al.*, 1928: 40–4]

In this way, the household survey data was processed in order to carry out a class analysis. Like the approach using money values, the points system approach allowed both the placing of households into class groups, and was flexible enough to achieve a balance between the different class tendencies that many households displayed. By expressing different relations on a common scale of points it was still possible to allow one set of class tendencies to strengthen or modify another in determining a household's overall character.

For example, a household which hired a labourer for 20 days and leased out 25 roubles' worth of stock in a year would be accorded respectively +3 points and +2 points. Each of these scores by themselves would indicate a small producer household with tendencies towards entrepreneurial activity. However, added together the score of +5 points would indicate a semi-capitalist farm. Thus each score would strengthen the other to determine the overall class character of the household. Two minus scores together would similarly reinforce each other to reveal a proletarian household.

On the other hand, contradictory points scores would cancel each other out. For example, a household might hire a worker for 100 days in a year, thus showing clear signs of being a semi-capitalist farm, but it might also have hired simple items of stock (−1 point) and have sold nine days of labour power (−1 point), thereby reducing its overall score to +3 points, making it a small producer farm with entrepreneurial tendencies. The range of possible permutations allowed in the scheme was extensive, and Kritsman, in his introduction to the research report, calculated that 85 different permutations were theoretically possible [*Vermenichev et al.,* 1928: 42–3, ix–x].

Using the approach outlined above, the research produced results which gave a breakdown of the sample as shown in Table 9 below. As can be seen from this table, with only minor irregularities, the figures showed a general situation where the higher the class grouping of a household, the more labour it hired, the more extra land it rented and the more stock and working animals it leased out. Conversely, the lower the class grouping, the more labour power a household sold, the more of its own land it leased out, and the more stock and animals it was obliged to hire.

The research team clearly felt their approach had been vindicated by the clarity of the results obtained but, at the same time they also pointed to further improvements which could be made. While they thought their system of classification had proved to be more accurate than others, using different indicators, they were still some way from clearly identifying classes in the countryside. In common with other applications of Kritsman's ideas, what they had delineated were class groups, that is groups sharing certain class tendencies or characteristics. Two further lines of enquiry seemed also to be necessary, they argued, in order to verify the degree to which the class characteristics revealed by their research corresponded to information about peasant life. First, it was necessary to analyse in detail the character of relations between the different groups they had identified, and to examine the precise nature of social and economic differences between them. Secondly, a further means of classifying households was needed to complement the scheme described above, which would show the extent to which a farm had a firm enough basis for accumulation or a weak enough basis that it would really be a candidate for proletarianisation [*Vermenichev et al.,* 1928: 45].

a. Social Relations and Production Characteristics of the Groups Within the Peasantry

For the groups we have arrived at to qualify as class types, it is necessary to analyse the character of their social relations and to examine a whole

TABLE 9

CHARACTERISTICS OF FARMS IN EACH CLASS GROUP

% of each class group

Class group	% of farms in the sample	hiring workers		selling labour		renting land		leasing out land		hiring stock or animals	leasing out stock or animals
		daily	seasonally	daily	seasonally	up to 2 *des.*	more than 2 *des.*	up to 30% of arable	more than 30% of arable		
I	10.3	4.3	—	31.4	68.6	1.4	—	30.0	42.9	85.7	12.9
II	22.4	7.9	—	41.5	2.6	2.0	—	26.3	9.9	94.7	13.8
III	40.4	29.7	0.7	7.4	—	14.3	1.1	7.0	3.3	84.9	48.0
IV	18.9	54.0	10.9	3.1	—	38.3	12.5	6.3	—	67.1	83.6
V	8.2	26.8	67.9	5.4	—	37.5	39.5	3.6	1.8	42.8	94.6

[*Vermenichev et al.*, 1928: 44]

series of economic differences between one type and another; only after this can we proceed with scientific validity to make clear the quantitative relations of class types and to establish their character [*Vermenichev et al.,* 1928: 45].

With this end in mind the authors, having set out their methods and discussed some problems entailed in them, went on to a detailed examination of peasant social relations in their chosen area. They devoted separate chapters to detailed descriptions of the hire and sale of labour power in agriculture, the hire and lease of stock and animals, rent relations, credit relations, forms of collective organisation in peasant agriculture, agricultural cooperation and wine production. Providing a wealth of figures, they tried to give support to Kritsman's account, drawn from his review of earlier Soviet peasant studies, where he had portrayed peasant farming as permeated by exploitative relations, and argued that truly independent farming was a rarity.

Following Kritsman, Vermenichev and his colleagues saw exploitative relations as offering opportunities for some households to begin a process of capital accumulation while others were increasingly proletarianised. However, also in line with Kritsman's ideas, they pointed to counter-tendencies, which to some extent they could identify in the Samara countryside, which meant that exploitative relations would not necessarily lead to a rapid take-off of capitalist development:

> We can expect a fairly clear-cut division of different socio-economic types at the extreme ends. Along with this . . . we must always keep in mind also the general situation in which this stratification proceeds, and which . . . is distinctly different from the conditions of stratification under capitalism. The nationalisation of land, of basic means of production in industry and transport, of the sources of credit, and co-operative development all give the proletarian state the possibility of strengthening its economic influence on agriculture in the direction of its socialist reconstruction [*Vermenichev et al.,* 1928: 122]

However, despite such general influences on agriculture, the immediate situation was still one where the possibilities for exploitation, and therefore class differentiation, were growing. Even if capitalism was not clearly emerging in the short term, clear differences between groups were becoming noticeable in various aspects of their existence. Vermenichev and his colleagues went on to examine a number of aspects of household structure and production to show how groups displayed regular differences from each other. These could be seen in family size and structure, in patterns of land use and crop cultivation, ownership of various means of production, sources of non-agricultural employment and patterns of involvement in the market.

Differences in household size and structure are shown in Table 10 below. Households in more capitalist-oriented groups tended to be bigger and were far less likely to be without male workers than households in more proletarian-oriented groups. This latter fact probably reflected the ravages of war which had weakened a number of households and contributed to their proletarian-isation by depriving them of young men.

TABLE 10

HOUSEHOLD SIZE AND STRUCTURE IN DIFFERENT CLASS GROUPS

Class group	No. in family	Workers on family farm per 100 pop.		% of households without male workers
		Male	Female	
I	4.8	19.5	31.0	25.7
II	4.9	23.1	27.3	11.2
III	5.2	21.5	25.5	6.6
IV	5.9	23.2	22.4	4.7
V	6.8	19.9	21.0	1.8
Average		22.2	25.3	8.8

[*Vermenichev et al.*, 1928: 125]

Households in the middle of the range tended to have slightly more male workers than households in extreme groups, but female workers were more numerous in lower-class households. In the semi-capitalist group V there was a slightly lower proportion of both male and female workers than in groups beneath them. Such tendencies may well have been accounted for by the possibility for more family members of not working on the farm in the higher groups than in the lower groups.

Further significant differences were noted in patterns of landholding. Households whose lands had been consolidated into single units separate from the communal arrangements of the rest of the village were much more common

TABLE 11

PATTERNS OF LANDHOLDING IN DIFFERENT CLASS GROUPS

Class group	Forms of landholding						Membership of an artel	
	Obshchina		Otrub		Khutor			
	% farms	% land	% farms	% land	% farms	% land	% farms	% land
I	94.3	91.3	4.3	7.6	—	—	1.4	1.1
II	92.1	89.8	5.3	8.2	—	—	2.6	1.1
III	88.2	81.7	5.5	10.2	1.5	2.6	4.8	5.6
IV	85.9	82.2	7.0	9.7	1.6	2.9	5.5	5.2
V	71.4	58.2	12.5	11.4	—	—	16.1	30.4
Average	87.9	80.0	6.2	9.8	0.9	1.6	5.0	8.6

[*Vermenichev et al.*, 1928: 127]

in more capitalist-oriented groups, as also was membership of a cooperative production unit.

More capitalist oriented groups were also shown to have more land at their disposal for cultivation, and to have made more extensive use of it. As can be seen from Table 12 below, a higher proportion of arable land was actually sown by upper class groups than lower class groups. This was explained partly by the fact that more upper class households had consolidated lands rather than the small strips with narrow margins between them to allow access which decreased the area of land actually sown in the *obshchina* system, and partly by the fact that the upper groups rented more land and in doing so only rented the amount of land they wished to sow and not the fallow which accompanied it.

TABLE 12

EXTENT OF CULTIVATION IN DIFFERENT CLASS GROUPS

Class group	Sowing per farm (in *des.*)	% of all own arable land actually sown
I	2.72	58.4
II	3.20	61.5
III	4.07	66.1
IV	5.87	72.5
V	10.57	81.0

[*Vermenichev et al.*, 1928: 127]

When it came to the pattern of crops sown however, the differences between groups were not nearly so marked as might have been thought. Although Table 13 below shows some differences between groups, notably that upper groups devoted more of their sowing to oats and grasses, (and in the case of group V also to sunflower seeds while sowing significantly less rye), the size of such differences would not seem to suggest radically different forms of production organisation or orientation to the market between groups. The researchers explained this as a result of the influence of the *obshchina* on production. Only when a farmer had consolidated fields, they argued, and when he had the freedom to cultivate what and how much he wanted, could he make any far-reaching changes. Within the *obshchina* the communal rules limited the extent to which changes were possible. Although a household could extend its cultivation by renting land, there was no incentive to make long-term improvements on rented land, and in any case, rented land was still subject to communal rules governing the rotation of groups in the three-field system prevalent in the area. Although some changes were possible, for example by using improved seeds and fertiliser, new crops, different patterns of weeding and improved machinery, if such changes were introduced on some strips while the neighbouring strips continued to be farmed by old methods, the extent and efficacy of the changes was likely to be limited.

The researchers attempted to provide support for their argument by referring to the information contained in the bottom line of Table 13 (group Va) on the sowing of the 14 households (25 per cent) of the semi-capitalist group V which had split off from the commune. The cultivation of these farms showed greater differences from the general pattern than did the cultivation of group V as a whole, signifying the more extensive changes in production organisation of farms beginning to develop as capitalist enterprises rather than simply expanding their sowing or building up surpluses of means of production for leasing out.

TABLE 13

SOWING OF EACH CROP AS % OF THE TOTAL SOWING OF EACH GROUP

% Crops

Class groups	Rye	Wheat	Oats	Millet	Other grains	Potatoes	Sun-flower	Flax Hemp	Grasses	Others
I	33.7	46.1	3.7	4.2	—	4.1	5.1	1.6	—	1.5
II	36.1	43.7	5.5	3.9	0.5	3.2	5.5	1.0	—	0.6
III	35.1	44.8	6.8	3.2	0.1	3.2	4.6	1.3	0.03	0.8
IV	35.8	41.6	8.2	2.4	0.3	2.4	4.6	1.5	0.5	2.7
V	26.8	45.8	10.2	2.5	0.1	2.0	6.1	0.8	4.6	1.1
Va	20.7	35.0	14.1	2.4	—	1.8	9.1	—	12.3	—

[*Vermenichev et al.*, 1928: 128]

In contrast to the data on crops, the figures for the ownership of animals and stock showed clear differences between the groups. As shown in Table 14 below, not only did the upper groups own more horses than their weaker neighbours (and some of their weaker neighbours, including 44.3 per cent, of group I, owned none at all), but the more entrepreneurial a farm, the more likely it was to have younger horses and more valuable horses. Such farms also owned greater quantities and higher values of farm stock, the differences here being much wider than for horses. Taking into account the greater ownership of animals and stock among the upper groups and the high proportions of farms without key means of production in the lower groups, the scope for exploitation between households can clearly be seen.

As well as providing information on issues which were central to the approach proposed by Kritsman and Nemchinov, the Samara study was notable for its breadth of scope, including information also on other aspects of peasant life and production. Unusually in Russian peasant studies, the Samara survey produced quite detailed information on non-agricultural employment, both on the 18 households in the sample where agriculture was not the main source of income, and on subsidiary non-agricultural occupations of households which were mainly dependent on agriculture.

As with some of the other studies of the Agrarian Marxist writers, the Samara researchers attempted to find a way of incorporating non-agricultural

TABLE 14

OWNERSHIP OF ANIMALS AND STOCK IN EACH CLASS GROUP

	Class Groups				
	I	II	III	IV	V
Av. no of working horses per farm	0.63	0.95	1.4	1.78	2.39
Young horses as % of all horses	18.2	17.4	22.0	26.3	28.4
Foals as % of all horses	6.8	7.6	10.5	9.2	10.5
Av. value of a working horse in roubles	97.7	118.1	123.4	138.3	170.0
% of farms without machinery or implements	62.8	36.2	13.9	—	—
% without ploughing equipment	77.1	55.9	28.9	8.6	7.1
% without advanced equipment	87.1	80.2	48.0	14.1	3.6
% without farm buildings	32.7	11.4	6.3	—	—
Av. value of equipment per farm in roubles	54.9	71.5	119.7	187.7	368.5

[*Vermenichev et al.*, 1928: 131–2]

activities into their classification of households. Of the households where agriculture was only a subsidiary activity, four were placed in group I as proletarians. These were the families of workers in the wine factory or on the railway. In group II were placed three households of small handicraftsmen (one stovemaker and two joiners), who sold labour for part of the year and leased out their land to more prosperous farmers. The remaining 11 households were a mixture of small traders and professionals who also cultivated their plots, often with the help of hired labour. According to the extent of their means of production and of their involvement in the hire or sale of labour power, they were mostly put in group III, with two each in groups IV and V.

Among the households with subsidiary non-agricultural activities, the researchers found that entrepreneurial activities such as miller and carrier were concentrated in group V along with those engaged in professional work. Small craftsmen such as blacksmiths and carpenters were mainly in groups II, III and IV, and part-time non-agricultural wage-workers were mainly in groups I and II [*Vermenichev et al.,* 1928: 133].

The researchers did not develop their discussion of non-agricultural activities any further and so, unfortunately, they offered no real analysis of non-agricultural activities as a source of capital accumulation. However, in the context of their time, the limited discussion in the Samara study stood out. In general, in both its scope and depth the Samara study promised well for the work the Agrarian Marxists might have gone on to do if they had had the chance. As can be seen from the figures provided above, the Samara researchers were not simply concerned to replace stratification indices with an improved index of class position, but they sought to explore the extent to which emerging class relations permeated peasant production. By examining the organisation of peasant production in the context of the relations of exploitation peasant farms were engaged in, they tried to establish to what extent either capitalist forms of organisation of farming were developing, or exploitation continued through the relations of a petty commodity economy.

As such it was the first detailed study of peasant society in a chosen area of the countryside which not only experimented with new methods of identifying class tendencies, but also used the approach it was developing to classify peasant households and organise empirical findings within the framework of its classification. It was the first study to offer detailed descriptions of the characteristics of different groups within the peasantry defined by their class tendencies rather than their position on a scale of stratification. In all this it was a very valuable piece of work.

b. The Identification of Classes Within the Peasantry

The main methodological concern of the Samara research, like the Volokolamsk research before it, was to identify and measure the extent of exploitation between peasant households, to classify households in terms of their overall balance between exploiting and dependent tendencies and thereby to make a judgement about the likelihood of capitalist farming emerging. The Volokolamsk researchers had not attempted to go any further than this. But, as was noted above, Nemchinov had suggested that the study of class formation could be taken one stage further by also classifying households by a measure of their economic strength as a means of assessing the likelihood of an exploiting position providing a basis for accumulation, or an exploited position providing the basis for proletarianisation. Like Nemchinov, and in contrast to the Volokolamsk study, the Samara study tried to incorporate such a second classification of households:

> Since the starting point for the formation of class groups is a concentration of the means of production by one group and the separation of these means of production from another, then it is quite clear that the analysis of production relations for the determination of class types must be conducted in connection with an analysis of the economic strength of different types, and only a combination of these two indicators – production relations and economic strength – can guarantee us the most well-founded results [*Vermenichev et al.,* 1928: 45].

The particular indicator chosen to represent the economic strength of households was the total value of all basic means of production, excluding land owned by a farm. In this they differed from Nemchinov who had used annual expenditure on constant capital. The reason for their choice was, the researchers argued, that it reflected well the main operations of the farm, that is both its expenditure of labour and its extent of land use. Other possible indicators considered were the size of a farm's annual income and the total value of a farm's production, but figures on these were less easily available and, it was thought, were more subject to fluctuation, and therefore less reliable as measures of a farm's strength as opposed to its particular performance at a given time.

Having acquired their figures, the farms in their sample were then classified into four groups according to the value of their means of production. The proportions of the sample in each group were as follows: group a) up to 250 roubles – 32.0 per cent; group b) 251–500 roubles – 31.4 per cent; group c) 501–1000 roubles – 27.0 per cent; group d) more than 1000 roubles – 9.6 per cent.

This grouping was used to modify the results of the grouping based on relations of exploitation in order to give a clearer picture of the farms actually in a position to accumulate or to become proletarianised. By cross-classifying the two groupings, the groups defined in terms of the value of their means of production were found to be distributed among the 'class groups' as follows:

TABLE 15

COMPARISON OF GROUPINGS BY DIFFERENT INDICATORS

Groups by value of means of production	% Class Groups				
	I	II	III	IV	V
a) Up to 250R	81.4	54.6	26.7	3.1	—
b) 251–500R	12.9	35.5	39.2	31.4	5.4
c) 501–1000R	5.7	7.9	30.8	45.2	44.6
d) More than 1000R	—	2.9	3.3	20.3	50.0

[*Vermenichev et al.*, 1928: 46]

A comparison of this kind was able to show two things. First, it was able to provide further support for the argument made several times already by the Agrarian Marxists that there were wide differences between the results of 'indirect' indices and 'direct' indices of class relations. Secondly, it could be used to refine the results of the survey to identify more clearly classes rather than groups with class tendencies. On this basis group V was split into a class of petty capitalists and a group of semi-capitalist households. At the other end of the scale, group I was split into proletarian and semi-proletarian households depending on whether wage labour was or was not the chief source of household income. The final classification of agricultural households produced by the research is shown in Table 16 below.

Of the 710 households in the sample, 679 were described as agricultural, that is, they made their living mainly by farming, while the remaining 31 were non-agricultural in that, although most of them continued to work their own plot of land, their main source of income was outside farming.

c. Kritsman on the Samara Research

While the Samara research was critically acclaimed as an empirical study of the peasantry of a particular region in terms of a class analysis, as noted above,

TABLE 16

THE MODIFIED CLASS GROUPS AND THEIR CHARACTERISTICS

Class group	% of total	Av. family size	Av. value of agricultural means of production	Av. head of cattle	Av. sowing (*in des.*)	selling labour	hiring labour	leasing out land	renting land	hiring stock and cattle	leasing out stock and cattle
										% of households	
Proletarian	1.4	4.6	62.4	0.2	1.18	100	0	100	0	80.0	0
Semi-proletarian	8.5	4.9	179.7	0.7	2.82	100	6.7	66.7	1.7	86.7	15.0
Small dependent	21.4	4.9	262.1	0.9	3.20	44.7	7.9	11.0	2.0	84.0	13.8
Small independent (neutral)	38.5	5.2	436.1	1.4	4.07	7.3	29.7	11.0	16.5	84.9	48.0
Small independent (entrepreneurial elements)	18.0	5.9	698.1	1.7	5.87	3.1	65.6	6.3	50.8	67.0	83.7
Semi-capitalist	7.9	6.8	1248.5	2.4	10.57	5.4	94.6	5.4	77.0	42.8	94.6
Petty capitalist	3.9	7.5	1809.8	2.8	14.72	1.2	96.5	3.0	82.1	28.6	96.4

[*Vermenichev et al.*, 1928: 138]

it should be seen primarily as a pilot study and as a part of the development of a new research approach to the class differentiation of the peasantry. As such, the Samara study was both welcomed and critically discussed by Kritsman who wrote an article reviewing the successes and the problems of the research, which was published as a foreword to the book.

In general Kritsman was positive about the results of the Samara researchers: 'The Samara expedition showed above all that . . . the question-naire produced was fully able to give an account of all the basic antagonistic social relations in the countryside' [*Kritsman,* 1928d: v]. In fact, Kritsman found the results sufficiently useful to analyse them himself and draw out various additional points to those made by the authors. He was particularly interested in figures relating to the hire of labour which he found to be useful for a refutation of the assumption, common among non-Marxist writers, that it was mainly households without able-bodied male workers which hired labour, and that therefore the hire of labour could not be taken as a sign of capitalist tendencies. In the Samara results, Kritsman found the following figures.

TABLE 17

HIRE AND SALE OF LABOUR AND THE ABSENCE OF MALE WORKERS

% of households without male workers

Among households both hiring and selling labour	28.6
Among households only selling labour for a season	26.7
Among households only selling labour of all types	16.5
Among households neither hiring nor selling labour	6.5
Among households only hiring labour of all types	6.4
Among households only hiring labour for a season	—

The higher levels of households without male workers selling their remaining labour power rather than hiring extra labour led Kritsman to the conclusion that: 'the lack of their own male workers does not lead (a household) at all to hire labour power from others, but, on the contrary, to sell its own labour power' [*Kritsman,* 1928d: vii].

More generally, the findings of the Samara study were of interest to Kritsman because, in a different way, they confirmed the findings of the Volokolamsk and Urals surveys, and Kritsman's own review of earlier literature, that the majority of peasant households (including the so-called independent producers) did not farm without engaging in transactions involving labour power, live or dead stock or land where they were either exploiting others or being exploited. However, the wealth of detail provided by the Samara research enabled Kritsman to draw out a further observation that, for the most part, the upper and lower groups were involved in transactions either with others in their own groups or with the other extreme group, while households in the middle group were mainly involved in transactions with each other [*Kritsman,* 1928d: xii–xiv].

Kritsman's main interest, however, was not in the details of the research findings but in the methodology. Although in many ways Kritsman thought the

Samara research had successfully achieved a class analysis of the kind he had suggested, this had not been achieved without problems. In general Kritsman found the grouping used to be 'cumbersome and lacking clarity' [*Kritsman,* 1928d: x]. Furthermore he listed a number of more particular criticisms.

First there was the problem of including rent and lease of land among the indicators of class tendencies where, Kritsman argued, the authors themselves had said that these transactions did not determine class relations. Echoing his earlier criticisms of Nemchinov, Kritsman clearly thought it illogical to use transactions involving land in the conditions of the 1920s when the land had only recently been redistributed and when land could not be bought and sold. In such conditions it did not seem to Kritsman that land could figure as an important basis for exploitation, even in areas of extensive grain cultivation [*Kritsman,* 1928d: x].

Secondly, it seemed particularly misleading to Kritsman to separate 'agricultural' from 'non-agricultural' households according to their main source of income. Instead, he argued, it should have been possible to account for the sale and hire of labour, whether in or outside agriculture, in the same terms. For example, a household might sell labour power for 30 days in a year to be employed in agriculture by other peasant households, which would be allocated -3 points, signifying a weak but not fully proletarian household. However, if the household also sold 20 days of labour power to industry or craft production, in a more 'comprehensive approach' the household could have been allocated extra minus points to make it clearly proletarian. Even if the failure to incorporate non-agricultural activities effectively in the scheme would not have made a vast difference to the Samara results, such possible sources of error needed to be eliminated bearing in mind possible further applications of the approach in areas where non-agricultural labour was more important.

Thirdly, Kritsman was unhappy about aspects of the method of allocating points. In some cases, he thought, the method adopted by the Samara researchers could give very misleading results and, in particular, incorporated a bias towards a large middle group of independent producers. For example, to take a rather extreme example, a household could hire 560 person-days of labour, thus giving $+5$ points, while at the same time, it could sell 60 days of labour power, thus giving -5 points. The balance of points in this case would be 0, indicating an independent petty-commodity producing household, whereas in reality it would be more likely to be a capitalist farm making extensive use of hired labour. For Kritsman the problem lay in treating the hire and sale of labour separately from each other. If a balance was taken of the number of days of hire and sale before the points were allocated, the balance would be the number of days for which points would be allocated, in this case almost certainly indicating a capitalist farm.[5]

Finally, Kritsman declared the criteria for allocating points to be arbitrary. Why, for example, he asked, should the hire of labour power for 10 days, the leasing out of up to 10 roubles worth of stock and the rent of up to two *desyatins* of land all receive the same number of points? As noted above, the

Samara researchers did not offer much discussion of their reasons for the points scores they chose. For Kritsman their judgements were necessarily arbitrary because the only way they could have had a firm basis for making them would have been if they had had data on the values of gains and losses in various transactions between households. Such information would have required a detailed budget study and, although Kritsman did not make the point explicitly, presumably he felt that a research approach of the kind used in Samara would have to be accompanied by a smaller scale budget study to provide it with basic information for deciding classification criteria [*Kritsman,* 1928d: xi].

Despite the significance of the results of the Samara research, and the superiority of its approach to studies based on the use of indicators such as sown area or ownership of working animals, for Kritsman the Samara research in a sense, had still used indirect indicators. Households were assessed and classified according to, for example, how much labour they had hired, or stock they had rented. In itself such measures could only indirectly reflect the extent of value expropriated and they could not, therefore, provide direct measures of exploitation. Therefore, implicit here also, although not clearly stated by Kritsman, was the judgement that studies of the class differentiation of the peasantry needed to be based on the detailed results of budget studies [*Kritsman,* 1928a: 136; 1928d: xii].

In this context, a further criticism, not discussed by Kritsman, can also be introduced. The Samara research, based on a questionnaire survey, was heavily dependent on the judgements and memories of individual peasants as to how much of various factors they had bought, sold, hired, leased or rented. Again budget methods, especially where a peasant householder was required to keep some regular accounts during the year, might have overcome some of the problems with the reliability of the information that the Samara researchers faced. Even without accounts kept regularly during the year, the greater detail of budget figures could have provided some kind of check on the opinions of householders reflected in the wider-based household survey.

However, the various criticisms of the Samara research should be seen in the context of a continuing collective enterprise, involving various trial surveys, with the general aim of refining methods of studying class relations and class structure in peasant agriculture.[6] Further progress would not have been possible without the lessons drawn, positive and negative, from studies like those in Samara and Volokolamsk. As suggested above, on a number of counts, the Samara research can still be seen as a landmark in the development of Soviet rural sociology.

The above studies have been discussed in detail in order to illustrate the approach of Kritsman and his colleagues, the range of methods under trial, and the problems they encountered in attempting to find the best indices of rural class relations. A few other studies of particular regions were carried out by members of the group in the 1920s [*Naumov and Shardin,* 1928; *Sulkovskii,* 1930], and although Sulkovskii's work in particular matched the Samara study in its interest and wealth of detail, no final decisions were made on all the discussions of method.

7. STUDIES USING MASS SURVEY DATA

Kritsman and his colleagues probably hoped for the application of their approach on a much larger scale and perhaps its incorporation into the nationwide surveys of the Ts.S.U. Indeed, towards the end of the 1920s, two leading members of the group, Nemchinov and Gaister, were already experimenting in this direction. Nemchinov, after his Urals research, turned his attention to reforms in the organisation of mass household censuses, and the dynamic surveys[7] in particular. He advocated a change from the use of 'natural indicators' such as sown area, to 'value indicators' which would give a value expression of the capacity of any given farm. Nemchinov's suggested approach involved two parallel groupings of farms, one using the total value of a household's means of production as its indicator, in order to measure the economic strength of a farm, and the other, a purely qualitative grouping to attempt to classify farms into class types. This second grouping used a combination of indicators including the hire and sale of labour, the hiring and letting out of animals and stock, the extent of sowing and the nature of engagement in *promysly*[8] by households. However, given the nature of the data available on the mass household censuses, none of these indicators of possible class tendency could be quantified.

While it can be argued that Nemchinov had devised the best approach possible in the circumstances for the analysis of mass data, nevertheless, it still contained many of the general problems with the use of indirect indicators. Moreover, unlike his earlier scheme used in his Urals research, a quantitative classification using an indirect indicator was now given priority and a purely qualitative classification was to be used to modify its results. In the Urals research, a typological classification of class types had been given priority.

Secondly, there was a particular problem with the intervals chosen by Nemchinov to distinguish groups of different economic strengths. The particular bands chosen by Nemchinov were: (i) without means of production; (ii) total value of 1–200R; (iii) 201–400R; (iv) 401–800R; (v) 801–1600R; (vi) more than 1600R. The same intervals were to be used for all regions and types of farming, the main stipulation being that the richest and poorest farms in a given band according to the value of their means of production should not have a total value more than double the corresponding farms in the group below them [*Nemchinov, 1928a*: 112]. Clearly, this was a rather arbitrary formulation revealing the abstract nature of the stratification it produced, not clearly related to existing relations and conditions in any particular region or locality.

Thirdly, in relation to the qualitative classification, the lack of any quantitative element in this scheme meant not only that the extent of any particular household's class tendency could not be indicated, but also that there was no way of measuring which was the dominant class tendency in households with mixed and contradictory characteristics. Given the large number of such households revealed by other Agrarian Marxist research, this must have been a major weakness.

A similar approach to analysing mass census data, entailing similar problems can be seen in the work of A. Gaister. While on a smaller scale than the nationwide dynamic census which Nemchinov was concerned with, Gaister's work was in some ways more interesting because he used his scheme of classification as the basis for a study of various social and economic characteristics of the Soviet peasantry, thus going beyond the more methodological concerns predominant in Nemchinov's work.

Alongside his participation in the Samara research, Gaister's other main contribution to Agrarian Marxist research was his leading role in analysing the social structure of the peasantry on a wider scale using data from peasant budget surveys carried out by the Ts.S.U. in 1925–6. In all, this study analysed 1242 peasant budgets in different regions of the USSR, including the North Caucasus, the steppe and forest-steppe regions of the Ukraine, Novosibirsk *okrug,* Smolensk *guberniya* and Tambov *guberniya.* The data gave a detailed and comprehensive picture of peasant production and inter-household relations in a varied range of agricultural regions. Gaister's book contained seven main chapters, giving a survey of the results of the agrarian revolution, a discussion of peasant farm income, an analysis of differences in the structure and organisation of farms in different class groups within the peasantry, and discussions of the rent and lease of land, the hire and lease of cattle and stock, the hire and sale of labour power, and the interrelations of classes and groups in the countryside.

In conducting his analysis, Gaister used two different groupings of households. First, he used an indicator of the economic strength of households, classifying them into strata according to the total value of their means of production, and secondly, he classified them into class groups in terms of their predominant relations of exploitation.

The first grouping yielded five groups:

(i) smallest farms with up to 200R in their means of production
(ii) small farms with 201–500R in their means of production
(iii) middle farms with 501–800R in their means of production
(iv) upper-middle farms with 801–1400R in their means of production
(v) large farms with more than 1400R in their means of production

[*Gaister,* 1928a: 25]

Apart from sharing similar economic positions, Gaister also suggested that households in the same group shared social characteristics in terms of their sources of income. While in smaller households wage labour was an important source of income, in middle and large households income from their own farm was more important, and in larger households the significance of income from leasing out cattle and stock also increased. In general, in terms of relations likely to give rise to class differentiation, Gaister found that 'the middle groups

of farms are characterised by the least spread of antagonistic relations'
[*Gaister,* 1928a: 24].

For his second grouping Gaister followed the by now established lines of
Agrarian Marxist research, using data on inter-household relations for his
indicators. However, unlike the previous studies, where the surveys had been
designed with Kritsman's approach in mind, Gaister had to use the data
available from the Ts.S.U. budget studies and was consequently more limited
in his choice of indicators. On the basis of the available information, Gaister
devised the following scheme:

  A. *Proletarian and semi-proletarian households*
    I. Proletarian households selling labour for more than 50 days.
    II. Semi-proletarian (*bednyak*) households selling labour for 20–50
        days, hiring animals for more than 20 days, hiring stock for more
        than 10 days.
  B. *Independent Producers (serednyaks)*
    III. *Serednyak* households selling or hiring labour for up to 20 days,
         hiring or leasing out cattle for up to 20 days, hiring or leasing out
         stock for up to 10 days.
    IV. Entrepreneurial households hiring labour for 20–50 days, leasing
        out cattle for more than 20 days, leasing out stock for more than 10
        days, renting more than two *desyatins* of arable land or more than
        five *desyatins* of meadow.
  C. *Small Capitalist Farms*
    V. Semi-capitalist and small capitalist (*kulak*) farms hiring labour for
       more than 50 days.

Using the more sophisticated data of budget surveys rather than household
surveys, Gaister was able to produce a more complex scheme than
Nemchinov's, incorporating some measure of the extent of different relations
if only in rather general units of time. However, the basis for Gaister's choice
of cut-off points between class groups was, as he admitted himself, somewhat
conditional. Without knowledge of all the local norms which would enable him
to determine to what extent the various transactions represented signs of
exploitation or dependence, Gaister was at a disadvantage compared with the
specific local surveys. His solution was to take as his guide the average figures
for each indicator of each of the five groups defined by the value of means of
production and the class groups he was attempting to identify. This point was
implied in his remark quoted above about households in the same stratum
sharing social as well as economic characteristics. Such an assumption,
however, must be highly debatable since, instead of making a break from
indirect indicators, Gaister was in fact using them to be able to introduce a
quantitative element into his direct indicators of class relations [*Gaister,*
1927b: 25–6; 1928a: 105–6].

Equally debatable was Gaister's next step. On the basis of the grouping
criteria described above, Gaister proceeded to develop a classification
of the agricultural population as a whole in four regions of the USSR:

the Ukraine (steppe and forest-steppe), the Urals, the North Caucasus, and Novosibirsk *okrug*. For this, Gaister extrapolated from his analysis of the peasant budgets to the Ts.S.U. dynamic household survey of 1925 which covered a total of around 21 million households. Gaister acknowledged that such an approach involved many problems but nevertheless, he thought it would give at least an approximate outline of the rural class structure of the Soviet Union. The results of this exercise are shown below in Table 18.

TABLE 18

% DISTRIBUTION OF CLASS TYPES

Class types		USSR	Ukraine	N. Caucasus	Urals *oblast*
I	Proletarian	7.3	16.5	19.3	10.8
II	Semi-proletarian	18.5	21.7	16.8	11.9
III	*Serednyak*	59.6	45.8	40.3	52.6
IV	Entrepreneurial	11.0	10.3	18.3	15.4
V	Semi- and small capitalist	3.6	5.2	5.3	9.3

[*Gaister*, 1927b: 28; 1928a: ch8; *Lewin*, 1968: 48]

The chief conclusion drawn by Gaister from his analysis was that the Soviet countryside was still overwhelmingly *serednyak*. The three sets of regional figures shown in Table 18 were for regions where class differentiation had proceeded further than the average for the USSR as a whole, and therefore in some regions, the proportion of *serednyak* households was higher than shown in the table [*Gaister*, 1927b: 29].

Using his classification of class types, Gaister then went on to explore various aspects of the production characteristics of the different classes. He was able to demonstrate clear shortages of animals and stock among the lower groups and concentrations of these factors among the upper groups. To a lesser extent there were also differences in sown area with the upper groups cultivating more land than the lower groups, per household. In general, for Gaister, his analysis of the situation confirmed the views of himself and his colleagues that the development of commodity production was giving rise slowly to the development of capitalist relations between households, widening the labour market, giving rise to proletarianisation and creating disparities in the distribution of means of production enabling significant exploitation between households.

Gaister's study, while based on a smaller population than Nemchinov's was able to produce a more sophisticated analysis thanks to the greater complexity of material available in the budget survey data he used. Also, following on the study of Samara, he was able to add further to the analysis of different aspects and problems of peasant farming presented explicitly in an organising framework which accepted a class-differentiated peasantry to exist. As such it provided some useful details and marked another step in building an alternative body of knowledge to be available to policy makers, economists and agronomists to that built up by the Organisation and Production School.

Given these qualities, recent commentators [*Solomon*, 1977: 107–9; *Lewin*, 1968: 48] and many contemporaries gave Gaister's work a generally favourable reception. However, it also attracted a number of criticisms. While it was praised as a worthy attempt to use the available mass data of the Ts.S.U. [*Kritsman*, 1928c: 342; *Popov*, 1928: 302] part of the value in doing this was seen to be that Gaister had identified certain problems both in the data and in the ways of analysing it rather than that the actual results obtained were necessarily valid as an account of the Soviet rural class structure as a whole.

As far as the Ts.S.U. budget data were concerned, it had not been collected with the purpose of class analysis in mind, and in many ways its categories were unsuitable for such a purpose. In his introduction to Gaister's book, Kritsman provided a useful background survey of the history of Russian agrarian statistics, showing how some of the concepts and understandings of peasant farming, which were still implicit in the Ts.S.U. figures, reflected ideological positions inimical to a Marxist class analysis [*Kritsman*, 1928c: 301–16]. As Kritsman pointed out, one of the chief of these understandings resulted in a tendency to concentrate on middle peasant households in the figures. Such a bias was clear in the figures used by Gaister where, according to Kritsman, the top and bottom groups in terms of value of means of production were both under-represented. Through a series of manipulations using other data from the Ts.S.U. surveys, Kritsman, in his introduction, attempted to assess the extent of such a bias in the figures used by Gaister [*Kritsman*, 1928: 317–32].

Moreover, echoing Kritsman's points, Naumov showed further ways in which the Ts.S.U. figures mystified class differentiation. Although an improvement on some earlier figures provided by the Ts.S.U. on the hire of labour, Naumov argued that the figures used by Gaister still mixed up transactions which would, in fact, have different class significance. Under one and the same category, were, for example, transactions involving the hire of workers on their own, which signified the proletarianisation of the seller of the labour power, and the hire of workers with their own working animals or stock, which, given the scarcity of means of production, was a sign of the exploitation of the 'buyer' of the labour power by the 'seller'. Also confused in the same category, Naumov argued, were pre-capitalist and family-cooperative forms of the exchange of labour [*Naumov*, 1928a: 208].

There were also criticisms of the way Gaister had analysed the figures. Whereas the figures themselves had been criticised for playing down differentiation, in some cases, it was thought, Gaister's approach had accentuated it to an unwarranted degree. For example, as Popov pointed out, Gaister's choice of sample regions was slanted to those of more extensive agriculture and the highest levels of commodity production, and therefore quite probably, higher levels of class differentiation.

Popov was also highly critical of Gaister's extrapolation from budget to mass household data. In general, he argued, extrapolation was one of 'the most imperfect statistical methods', and, in this case, its unreliability was particularly great because Gaister's sample was too small, and because Russian peasant households of the time were too mixed or contradictory in their internal structure to be able to generalise about them as clear types for the purposes of extrapolation. For Popov, the danger of Gaister's method of extrapolation was in over-accentuating the well-off and exploiting groups within the peasantry [*Popov*, 1928: 306].

The validity of Gaister's method of extrapolation was also criticised by Kritsman on other grounds. Kritsman expressed doubts about Gaister's assumption that there was sufficient correspondence between his two groupings to allow data from his grouping of strata by economic strength to determine the quantitative levels of his indicators of class group membership. A cross-tabulation of the two groupings showed that, although there were no cases where a household in the lowest group by one classification appeared in the highest group in the other classification, nevertheless, there was too little correspondence between the membership of groups at the same point on each scale for Gaister to be justified in his approach. It therefore seemed dangerous ground on which to build his extrapolation [*Kritsman*, 1928c: 355].

Gaister also received criticism for the low qualitative levels of his class group indicators which he held to be necessary to allocate a household to a particular group. For Naumov, for example, 50 days' hire of labour was in itself too little to classify a household as capitalist, and sale of 50 days' labour was insufficient to make a household necessarily proletarian [*Naumov*, 1928: 209]. Since these figures had been arrived at by taking the average levels of these transactions for the top and bottom groups in terms of value of the means of production, this was a further argument against Gaister's assumption that there was a sufficient correspondence between the two sets of classifications.

For Kritsman, given the type of data available to Gaister, all he could realistically do was to indicate in a conditional manner the class tendencies of households. Gaister, however, had made a serious error in presenting the classification, obtained through his highly conditional method, as representing the classes in their actual proportions in the Soviet countryside. At the present stage of its development the Agrarian Marxist approach, and especially the form of it developed by Gaister, could not go beyond identifying class tendencies within its chosen samples of households [*Kritsman*, 1928c: 333–4].

Gaister's presentation of his work as attempting a representation of the actual class structure of the Soviet peasantry attracted a good deal of attention, not only in research circles, but more widely, mainly because it was taken up and used by the Left Opposition. Gaister's claim to be identifying the extent of capitalist development in the countryside attracted the attention of the authors of the *Counter-Theses of the Left Opposition* to the XV Party Congress. On the basis of Gaister's description of groups of capitalist (group V) and entre-preneurial (group IV) households, they combined these two groups as an upper group developing into a capitalist class. This led Gaister to publish a further article denying the validity of the Left Opposition's interpretation of his work and stressing the *serednyak* nature of his group IV [*Gaister,* 1927c: 18].

In all, Gaister's work was found wanting in many aspects but the criticism it attracted from other researchers was partly a tribute to it, a sign of its recognition as an ambitious attempt to develop Kritsman's approach further and apply it to mass data. The critics also praised much in the wealth of detail Gaister provided and found it useful to learn from his mistakes. In the information it provided, it gave further support to Kritsman's view that in the particular conditions of the NEP capitalist relations were developing in unusual ways through the exploitation of ownership of scarce means of production. The study also provided further argument against the use of the old standard indicators in the study of peasant differentiation and for the potential of the new ones it was experimenting with. Although Gaister's particular solutions were also criticised, nevertheless they contributed to the methodo-logical debates not only about how to process existing material but about how future material could be made more appropriate to the needs of the research.

Fundamentally, the problem for all the approaches using mass survey data was that they were ambitious attempts to respond to political demands for more concrete analyses of the rural class structure when the available mass survey data was quite inadequate for such purposes. In this context it is important to judge the analyses attempted as contributions to a methodological debate which was beginning to come under more political pressure than hitherto. As Kritsman had noted, given the rudimentary development of the process of class formation which it was attempting to study, the research was only really capable of indicating class tendencies at its existing stage of development.

However, while the research of the Kritsman group, in all its many aspects,[9] offered a number of interesting possibilities for future research, and as such, retains much interest today, any further developments were to be overtaken by the event of Stalin's forced collectivisation of the peasantry. Discussion of the work of Kritsman and his colleagues became a taboo subject in the Soviet Union for many years and even now, although some modern Soviet writers have recognised Kritsman's originality [e.g., *Chagin,* 1971], the question of the possible continuing relevance of his work for peasant studies has not been raised.

8. THE THEORETICAL CONTRIBUTION OF THE AGRARIAN MARXIST RESEARCH

Apart from the particular criticisms or differences of opinion about each piece of research which have been discussed above, two issues of a more general theoretical nature emerge for discussion. The first concerns the question of the 'middle peasants' and how to classify them in class terms, and the second concerns the degree to which the groupings identified by research using direct class indices could actually be considered to be classes.

(i) Classification of 'Middle Peasants'

The studies varied in the way they grouped the farms in their samples into class categories. The Samara study (and also Gaister's study) had a middle category of farms which seemed to be tending neither towards proletarianisation nor towards capitalist development, but the Volokolamsk study did not make provision for such a group. In the Samara study the sample was classified into five groups with two tending towards capitalism and two towards proletarianisation, while the middle group showed no clear signs either of entrepreneurship or dependence. This middle group was made up of just over 40 per cent of the sample, a finding which provoked some criticism from Kritsman. In his view the criteria chosen for the grouping in the first place biased the results in favour of a large middle group.

Kritsman's own views predisposed him to regard with suspicion the argument that there was a large truly independent middle peasantry with all the connotations of self-sufficiency and being rooted in a natural economy that this term conveyed. Probably close to his own preferences was the scheme adopted in the Volokolamsk research, which played down the existence of a middle peasantry, and did not even accord them a separate grouping in their scheme. This is not to suggest, however, that Kritsman did not believe in the existence of a middle peasant group at all. The geographical situation of Volokolamsk (near Moscow and with a developed commodity economy based on flax as the main cash crop) meant that it was an exceptional area in the Soviet countryside where class differentiation could be expected to have proceeded further than in most other areas. In view of this it seemed reasonable to the Volokolamsk researchers to use a scheme in which even farms with only slight tendencies towards proletarianisation or capitalist development were placed in a group according to their dominant tendency, however weak. The researchers argued that this was justified since nearly all members of any potential middle peasant group showed signs of elements of dependence in their operations and could not be regarded as independent peasant farmers. For this they have been taken to task by one recent critic [*Solomon*, 1977: 103], who has argued that their categories set up a self-fulfilling prophecy: by excluding a middle peasant group to begin with, in analysing their data they successfully masked signs of one in their results.

However, although it may have been preferable to include an independent peasant grouping in their scheme, no matter how few households belonged to it, the charge of distortion inherent in Solomon's criticism goes too far. The problem with her interpretation, both on this specific question and on the work of the Agrarian Marxists in general, is that in attempting to locate the research in its social and political context she tends to lose sight of the theoretical basis of the research which provides the logic of the categories chosen. It will be argued below that an examination of Kritsman's theoretical approach helps explain the logic behind his suspicion of the concept of a middle peasantry.

(ii) Identification of the groupings produced by the research with social classes

Connected with the above issue is the question of the extent to which the groups of peasant farms produced by the methodologies of the Agrarian Marxists could be considered to be class groups within the peasantry. By the end of the 1920s, political pressures on the research began to favour attempts to actually identify such class groups (and especially a group of agrarian capitalists) within the peasantry and, as noted above, some researchers, especially Gaister, were prepared to attempt this, drawing criticism from Kritsman who argued that Gaister's methodology could only indicate tendencies towards class formation within the groups of the peasantry identified [*Kritsman,* 1928c: 342].

Such comments by Kritsman have led Solomon to suggest that there are contradictions in Kritsman's approach between the early articles which prompted research such as the Volokolamsk study where he argues that an independent middle peasant group are insignificant in the Soviet countryside, and the slightly later criticism of Gaister which, according to Solomon, argues against a clear identification of rural class formation and for the continuing significance of a middle peasantry. However, on closer view, what Kritsman actually says in his criticism of Gaister is that the peasantry remain largely petit-bourgeois in class nature despite elements of proletarianisation and capitalism within them [*Kritsman,* 1929: 342]. In other words, he was saying that the groups which could be singled out for their entrepreneurial or dependent characteristics were still made up of basically petit-bourgeois small commodity producers.

On both this issue and the question of the middle peasantry the key to Kritsman's ideas is the third concept, implicit in his work, of class relations which in themselves only imply tendencies towards class formation as opposed to the more concrete concepts of classes on the one hand or strata on the other. Most of the debate on the differentiation of the peasantry was conducted through the medium of these latter concepts, whereas Kritsman's originality lay especially in his pioneering of the former.

9. KRITSMAN AND THE THEORY OF CLASS RELATIONS WITHIN THE PEASANTRY

First of all, in order to understand the originality of Kritsman's ideas it is necessary to locate his work in the context of early Soviet Marxist attempts to theorise the nature of the social structure of Soviet society in the first decade of its existence.

Most influential on Kritsman were the first tentative attempts of Lenin to analyse the balance of class forces through which the Bolshevik government aimed to steer a course in developing socialism. Along with other early Soviet theorists, such as Preobrazhenskii, Kritsman was interested in following up Lenin's concern with the question of the existence and interrelation of different structures or systems of production which all coexisted in the complex social formation of Soviet society. Unlike the Britain of Marx's *Capital* or even the France of his *18th Brumaire* it was more difficult to conceptualise the Soviet social formation as determined by any one mode of production. Lenin in fact described it as a transitional society, neither capitalist nor socialist. In his pamphlet, 'On the Tax in Kind' which inaugurated the NEP, Lenin listed five 'structures' making up the Soviet social formation:

1. patriarchal economy, (self-sufficient peasant 'natural' economy)
2. petty-commodity economy (independent small commodity producers)
3. capitalist economy (expanded reproduction for profit and the sale of labour power)
4. socialist economy (planned by the proletarian state)
5. state-capitalist economy (capitalist and petit-bourgeois enterprises under the general direction and control of the proletarian state)

[*Lenin*, 1921]

In addition, as Kritsman pointed out [1928a: 117] for some parts of the Soviet Union a sixth structure of feudalism could be added, especially for some parts of Central Asia.

The exact use to which such concepts would be put in a detailed analysis was never spelled out clearly either by Lenin or by Kritsman, but in general it is clear that the path of development of Soviet society was to be understood as the complex result of the inter-penetration of those structures in each other. Each in a pure form would presuppose a given mode of expropriation of the surplus and a given pattern, consequently, of class relations. In the interrelation of different structures a number of different patterns of class relations would be theoretically possible but the more dominant structure could be expected in time to undermine the weaker ones to impose a pattern of class relations more similar to those prevailing in the pure form of the dominant structure. This, however, would be long-term development and in the early stages of development of a transitional society the patterns of class relations could be both very complex and quite fluid.

Prior to the Bolshevik Revolution Marxist theory would have invariably identified capitalism as the structure likely to achieve dominance within a transitional society as capitalist development took place increasingly on a world scale. However, according to Lenin, the Bolshevik Revolution introduced the possibility of conscious intervention in economic relations by the socialist state in order to regulate and limit the growth of capitalist relations and foster the growth of more socialist forms of production and distribution. In other words, the Revolution had made possible a new combined structure of state capitalism. Although no immediate transition to socialism could result from the Revolution, a socialist state could institute policies to regulate capitalist tendencies in the economy, both in industry and in agriculture.

As far as the petty-commodity economy of the peasants was concerned, the reintroduction of the market under the New Economic Policy had given a boost to the possibilities of capitalist development in agriculture. Lenin, however, thought the state could operate through the institution of agricultural cooperatives to provide a non-capitalist large-scale socialised form of agriculture which could offer the peasants a more efficient and secure basis for their farming and distract their aspirations away from ideas of becoming big capitalist farmers [*Lenin, 1923*].

Until the end of the 1920s, Kritsman consistently maintained this vision of Soviet social development. On several occasions he professed faith in the power of state intervention to check the capitalist tendencies in peasant agriculture. In this sense, therefore, the study of potential capitalist relations within the peasantry was not the most significant question to be studied in Soviet society. It was, however, important to have accurate information on both the rate and the specific forms of capitalist development if effective policies were to be devised to counteract them, and in this lay the value of research on peasant class differentiation. Because the forms of this potential development were different in the post-revolutionary period it was important to spend a long time devising the correct methodology to grasp their new complexity [*Kritsman, 1928a:* 114–17].

According to this view Russian peasants were, on the whole, small commodity producers in a transitional society who might move, in terms of social relations, in any one of a number of different directions. They might move toward agricultural cooperation and thus to socialism; or through the cooperatives to capitalism; or directly to capitalism through the exploitation of their neighbours; or towards proletarianisation as they became increasingly dependent on their stronger neighbours to maintain their own production. As can be seen from the range of possibilities, the transition to capitalism was perfectly feasible, although for Kritsman not an imminent change in the 1920s. But the main point was the way the potential transition was to be conceptualised. For Kritsman the transition was taking place within each peasant household and each household contained its own complexity of contradictory tendencies. The aim of his research was to build up a general picture of the extent and strength of these tendencies.

It seems to me that this view is rather different from the usual conceptualisation of the transition and differentiation of the peasantry. It is usually seen much more in terms of concrete class-like groups or strata which are credited with a fairly firm existence. They are already identifiable as groups which are more or less internally homogeneous as far as their class relations are concerned. Such seems to be the conceptualisation of the problem in Lenin's pre-revolutionary work and basically it is the approach adopted by the orthodox post-revolutionary researchers such as Khryashcheva also. It tended to imply that peasant groups had already almost solidified, if not as classes then at least as interest groups, with their own separate interests which it would be difficult to change. Yet this is a view which for many close observers of Russian peasant society did not seem to tie in with the reality they knew. Some of the most acute of these observers reacted by an assertion of the social homogeneity of the peasantry in terms of class interests and by interpreting inequalities in terms of cyclical mobility. This was, of course, a reflection of reality, but a distorted one all the same, which ignored the exploitative relations basic to Kritsman's understanding of the peasantry. A closer approximation would be gained by conceptualising the peasantry as a category characterised by class relations permeating each household so that each family could move along different paths of class development according to the opportunities and incentives available.

Thus, what Kritsman's approach achieved was not evidence of the existence of classes but evidence of class relations between peasant households. Although in itself this approach could not resolve the question of the development of rural capitalism, it nevertheless made a substantial contribution to the debate on this question by showing that a process of expropriation of the agricultural surplus was taking place between peasant farms in a systematic way. This meant, at least, that there was emerging in Russian peasant agriculture an important necessary condition for the development of capitalist agriculture which also had the effect of cross-cutting any processes favouring the preservation of a more homogeneous peasant class.

Furthermore Kritsman's approach implied a critique of all existing ways of looking at the question of the class differentiation of the peasantry. Most basically his ideas question the existence of the category of independent self-sufficient peasants achieving their existence in a petty-commodity economy by almost exclusive use of their own household labour on their own farm. For Kritsman, the Russian peasantry was rarely independent in its relations of production since on any one farm one would be likely to find aspects of the family's farming operations in which it was exploiting the labour of outsiders, and other aspects in which it was exploited by outsiders. The central dynamic of Russian peasant society of this period was thus provided by the relations of expropriation of the surplus product between peasant households.

CONCLUSIONS

Although Kritsman and his colleagues were never able to apply their methodology to reach a fully satisfactory picture of the Soviet rural class structure in the 1920s, their work was very interesting for a number of reasons:

(i) They produced a highly sophisticated methodology for the study of peasant differentiation which went beyond deducing propositions about class relations from static indicators of inequality and produced insights into the processes and relations which actually produced the observed inequalities in peasant society.[10]

(ii) They developed a methodology which showed promise of providing precise information about the socio-economic relations between peasant households prevalent in Russian society at the time, which was needed for the more theoretical study of the question of the typification of the Soviet social structure [*Preobrazhenskii,* 1926: 208; *Kritsman,* 1925d; 1926b].

(iii) Although Kritsman and his colleagues believed the data produced by their approach to be evidence of the eventual long-term formation of a clear-cut agrarian bourgeoisie and proletariat, their methodology in itself would not necessarily prove this and indeed its application need not be limited to cases where such processes are occurring. The methodology is an open-ended one which does not necessarily presume its answers. It sets out to discover the extent of independent peasant farming on the one hand, and class differentiation (evidence of both exploitative and exploited farms) on the other. As such Kritsman's approach could be of use in understanding both the processes producing class formation and the processes producing a homogeneous peasantry.

(iv) In the case of Russia in the 1920s the Kritsman group's research suggested that very few households carried out farming completely independently and thereby raised doubts about the concept of a middle peasant as a self-sufficient independent farmer with different interests from rich and poor peasants. The concept of middle peasants can be seen as the product of a stratification approach to the question of peasant social structure and with the use of research based on direct class indicators the importance of the concept could well decline. It would be interesting to discover if similar results would be obtained from Kritsman's approach if it were applied in the study of modern peasantries.

NOTES

1. Clearly all this reflects the particular set of circumstances of peasant agriculture in the Soviet Union of the 1920s. A combination of the redistribution of the land with the scarcity of animals and farm implements created by both the disruption of war and the increase in households taking up farming, all produced a specific situation in which, given a petty commodity economy, owners of scarce animals and stock were able to exploit their strength. Obviously such conditions would not prevail in all, or even most peasant societies where land, or even labour might be more scarce and would therefore become more significant determinants of peasants' class positions. In such cases any equivalent of Table 1 for other societies would be rather different.

2. It should be noted that Solomon is incorrect in stating that the grouping in terms of prosperity of farms was based on a measure of income [1977: 97]. As noted above, Nemchinov's indicator was expenditure on constant capital.

3. It should be noted that there were some mistakes in the figures given in their articles by both Kritsman and Nemchinov. In both cases, corrected figures are given in the text here.
    For farm a) Kritsman mistakenly took the total value of the household's own means of production on their own farm to be R504.24 instead of R604.24. The value of all the household's means of production on 'own' farm was 97.9% of all 'own' means of production. As a result Kritsman calculated a figure of 49.9% for independent elements, and therefore of

50.1% for entrepreneurial elements.

For farm b) Nemchinov mistakenly calculated the farm to be 123.3% dependent.

4. It is unlikely that the low value of their labour power on their own farms would have been explained by an overall lack of labour power. The households, in this group did not have significantly fewer adults than those in the groups above them. All had at least one adult of each sex, and in some cases there were teenage children as well [*Anisimov et al.,* 1927: 89].

5. The team had decided (with Kritsman's approval) that days of labour sold and hired were not directly equivalent to each other in their significance for class relations. This is reflected in the different numbers of days which act as the same points equivalent for sale and hire. Therefore it must be assumed that Kritsman was not simply advocating subtracting 60 from 560 in the above example. Presumably the 60 days would have been weighted by some predetermined figure before the balance was taken.

6. In contrast to the view presented here, which has attempted to show the Samara research as one of a series of attempts to refine a research approach – each of which was examined critically by Kritsman and his school – Solomon has seen the Samara study as somehow the developed orthodox version of the Agrarian Marxist approach:

> The Samara study was significant for two reasons. First, it established a methodology for grouping peasant farms, *a methodology that was replicated with little variation in study after study* conducted by the Agrarian-Marxists; and second, the young agrarianists *considered the study's findings typical of social structure in the Soviet Union* and treated the Samara data as a base line against which the results of subsequent studies were compared [*Solomon,* 1977: 106].

I have not been able to find any evidence to support either of the assertions I have emphasised in the quote from Solomon above, and she has offered no support in her own book from which the quote was drawn.

7. The dynamic surveys were a particular form of household survey in which, as far as possible, exactly the same households were studied over a period of years instead of taking different samples from a given area at different dates.

8. *Promysly* were crafts, trades or outside work undertaken by members of a household, producing an income. This included various 'self-employed' or 'employer' activities as well as wage labour. Because the term was used for activities involving different kinds of relations, Marxist writers found its use by statisticians misleading. However, until well into the 1920s Soviet agrarian statistics continued to use this category. For the debate on the precise meaning of the term, see Shanin [1975] and Smith [1975].

9. In the second half of the 1920s the Agrarian Marxists branched out into a number of areas of research other than the class differentiation question. These included work on changes in the internal relations of peasant households, the character of collective agriculture and the development of a Marxist approach to agricultural economics as a discipline. However, compared with their research on class relations these other areas were still in the early stages of development by the time all the group's research was brought to an end.

10. For a rather different interpretation of Agrarian Marxist research (in particular of Nemchinov, as well as brief references to Kritsman and Gaister) see T. Shanin, 'Measuring Peasant Capitalism', in E. Hobsbawm, *et al.* (eds.), *Peasants in History* (Oxford, 1980), especially pp. 92–7.

Shanin has also reproduced versions of Tables 1, 2 and 3, above. In contrast to his rather negative view of Agrarian Marxist work in *The Awkward Class,* his appraisal here, particularly of Nemchinov (the only Agrarian Marxist he discusses in detail) is very positive.

However, it seems to me that Shanin's account is somewhat misleading on two main counts. First, he presents Nemchinov rather in isolation from the work of other Agrarian Marxists, and from Kritsman in particular. This obscures the degree of influence Kritsman had in general terms on Nemchinov's thinking and moreover, ignores Kritsman's further discussion and adaptation of Nemchinov's Urals research approach. This is important because in many important respects it was Kritsman's adaptation, rather than Nemchinov's own approach which was most influential on the subsequent surveys carried out by the Agrarian Marxists.

Secondly, Shanin obscures the novelty of the work of the Agrarian Marxists, and notably Nemchinov, in pioneering research using direct measures of relations of exploitation between households as indicators of potential class formation, rather than, the more usual indirect stratification indicators. For example the only work by Kritsman which Shanin refers to explicitly is the work of a commission studying the agrarian revolution, edited by Kritsman, which given the nature of the data available on that period, was obliged to use indirect stratification indicators. Similarly, Shanin refers to Gaister's stratification approach in his 1928 study, but not to the alternative approaches of, for example, the Volokolamsk or Samara studies. Even in the case of Nemchinov, although Shanin produces the tables showing Nemchinov's use of direct indicators of exploitation, Shanin does not make the point explicitly that it was in pioneering their use that Nemchinov's novelty primarily lay.

II. The Agrarian Marxist Research in its Political Context; State Policy and the Development of the Soviet Rural Class Structure in the 1920s

Gary Littlejohn*

INTRODUCTION

Developments in the Soviet Union of the 1920s have been the object of renewed interest in recent years, largely because various historical options were still open at that time and because of the high standard of debates in various arenas on how the Soviet Union should develop. The period of the New Economic Policy (NEP) from 1921 to 1929 is of particular interest, because NEP represented an attempt to construct a non-coercive socialist policy towards a peasantry which was not conceived of as a class or as a unified social force. The historically anti-democratic effects on the Soviet Union (and on world politics) of the failure of this attempt are extremely well known, at least in broad outline. There is a lot to be gained from the analysis of the reasons for this failure, both in terms of understanding the contemporary Soviet Union and in terms of the pertinence of the problems faced under the New Economic Policy to the contemporary problems of developing countries. This acknowledgement of the importance of the 1920s provides the justification for many of the studies of that period, yet precisely because of the complexity of these developments, the richness of the empirical sources and the high standards of the various debates, the contemporary debates in the West about the 1920s are still continuing. This contribution attempts to investigate some relatively neglected aspects of the debate, in the light of the growing view in some quarters that the policy of forced collectivisation of the peasantry was not only economically and politically unnecessary, but actually impeded the implementation of the first Five Year Plan.

The prevailing view among many shades of political opinion has tended to accept the terms of the Soviet industrialisation debate within the Bolshevik leadership as an adequate definition of the problems which the country then faced. A good example of this approach is the essay by Nove [1964]. The argument there accepts that the period of restoration of the economy from the ravages of civil war had passed by the latter 1920s, and that the reconstruction of the economy was reaching the point where further investment would have to

*University of Bradford and Centre of African Studies, Eduardo Mondlane University, Maputo.

be on a much greater scale than before if production was to continue growing at the same pace and if the country was to be industrialised. Since the majority of the population was engaged in agriculture, the investment funds would have to come from agriculture. Thus basically the investment would have to take place at the cost of a relative or even absolute decline in the incomes of the peasantry, with the 'surplus' being pumped into industry. Industrialisation under the direction of the Bolshevik Party thus almost necessitated forced collectivisation as a means of controlling the peasantry while the surplus was pumped out of agriculture. In this sense, if the Bolshevik Party were to retain power, Stalin probably was necessary, according to this line of reasoning. The main alternative view has tended to be that collectivisation was necessary in order to increase agricultural productivity beyond the limits set by small-scale peasant production, but that forced collectivisation, rather than voluntary collectivisation, was not only very costly in lives and highly detrimental to the whole political structure, but reduced the scale of the surplus that might otherwise have been extracted from the peasantry. The latter kind of argument has been common, for example, among Marxists of various persuasions. Briefly, then, most analyses have accepted that collectivisation was a precondition for socialist industrialisation because of the limitations of small-scale peasant agriculture. It has often been part of such arguments that without collectivisation any agricultural surplus would be under the control of small-scale rural capitalists or *kulaks* who would thus be in an economic position to challenge the Bolshevik control over the pattern of industrialisation. The main challenge in English to this latter point came (at least until the mid-1970s) from writers such as Chayanov [*Thorner et al.,* 1966] or Shanin [1972], who argued that the peasantry was not undergoing a process of substantial class differentiation along capitalist lines.

However, the terms of the debate were somewhat changed – even for those who might have been reluctant to accept arguments along the lines of Chayanov or Shanin – by the work of Barsov appearing in the Soviet Union itself which apparently demonstrated that the first Five Year Plan was carried through without the extraction of an agricultural 'surplus'. Not only had the real incomes of collective farm workers (*kolkhozniki*) declined, but agricultural deliveries to the towns and industry had also declined. Collectivisation had proved irrelevant to the process of industrialisation, in the sense that it did not deliver any agricultural 'surplus' for investment. The implications of this were already beginning to be registered in the well-known debate between J. Karcz [1967, 1970] and R. W. Davies [1970] on the 'grain problem' of the late 1920s, and were further discussed in Harrison [1978a], Hussain and Tribe [1981], and in Smith [1979].[1] The last two publications have criticised the conception of agricultural surplus involved in the previously prevailing terms of the debate, and have stressed the possibility of generating investment funds within the industrial sector itself by various means, including organisational improvements both in the planning process and in terms of the technical division of labour. The conclusion is that such changes must have been the main source of investment funds, since agriculture did not provide them. Such a conclusion has many implications, but the main one which will be pursued here is that it changes the terms in which developments in the class structure in the 1920s should be appraised. It also changes the terms of appraisal of state policy towards the rural class structure of the time.

Whatever changes in the class structure may have been registered by research or official statistics, one need no longer analyse them primarily in terms of their impact on the delivery of an agricultural surplus to provide the basis for an industrialisation programme. This is not to deny that the division of social production meant that agriculture supplied both raw materials to industry and consumer goods to the town, but the appraisal of the role of agriculture need not be conducted in the same terms as those used by the leadership and Left Opposition of the Bolshevik Party. In particular the development of capitalism within agriculture, with the supposed capacity of capitalists to control the delivery of the surplus by controlling its production, did not necessarily threaten to subvert the industrialisation programme, as most of the Bolshevik leadership increasingly came to believe.

The conceptualisation of industrialisation as requiring the extraction of an agricultural surplus (as a source of rapid accumulation) was prevalent in the 1920s, and its influence among later commentaries is evident. Yet the rejection of such a line of reasoning does not imply an indifference to the rural class structure of the 1920s, nor does it entail a denial of the view that collectivisation could have eased and speeded the process of industrialisation by providing additional sources of investment and consumption of goods. It simply means that these issues were not as critical for the development of socialism as the Bolshevik leadership came to believe, even though some form of industrialisation was a condition for the survival and development of socialism in the Soviet Union.

The conclusion that collectivisation was not a critical precondition for industrialisation can also be established on the basis of the analysis of the NEP itself by Grosskopf [1976]. A major conclusion to be drawn from her superb study is that the difficulties of the NEP at the end of the 1920s were due primarily to policy failure in implementing the NEP, so that the NEP itself did not constitute a major obstacle to the industrialisation programme. Grosskopf's work has been cited by Hussain and Tribe [1981] and by Smith [1979], but it also forms a major influence on the somewhat different work on the 1920s by Bettelheim [1978]. The reliance by Bettelheim on Grosskopf means that Part Two of Volume Two of his work is probably the best-known indication so far available in English of Grosskopf's arguments, but the positions of Grosskopf and Bettelheim should not be equated. Grosskopf's work does lend support to the analysis of the peasantry developed by Lenin towards the end of his life, but it is convincing because of its extensive use of primary empirical sources.[2] On the basis of an extremely detailed analysis of developments during the period of NEP, Grosskopf demonstrates that the *smychka,* that is the union or linking between the peasantry and the proletariat, was by no means economically moribund after the crisis of 1925–6 and that the later crisis of the NEP in 1927–8 was primarily due to the failure to 'learn the lessons' of the earlier crisis. This occurred despite the comparatively clear analysis of the problems by Dzerzhinsky prior to his death in 1926, so the failure was not an analytical one but a political one. A more rigorous pursuit of certain neglected aspects of the NEP, particularly of the supplying of means of production to the poor peasantry, would have substantially increased agricultural output, making industrialisation that much easier. Thus her analysis shows that the supposed 'limits' of small-scale production could be considerably extended by an appropriate policy of state support for the poor peasantry. More to the point, such support for the poor peasantry would have provided the economic conditions for voluntary forms of cooperation and collectivisation, that is it would have facilitated the undercutting of capitalist relations of production and the development of socialist relations. It is from this standpoint, rather than a concern with a surplus for industrialisation, that the class structure of the 1920s will be examined in this article.

However, despite the considerable importance of Grosskopf's work, it must be said that she devotes comparatively little space to the direct analysis of the processes of class differentiation of the peasantry. She concentrates instead on the appraisal of state policy towards the peasantry, on economic relations between agriculture and industry and on the economic effects of these on the production and distribution of agricultural produce, particularly grain. These in fact constitute the main social conditions of the processes of class differentiation (or lack of differentiation) among the peasantry, and Grosskopf refers to the main sources of research in her estimate of the extent of class differentiation, including Khryashcheva, Gaister, Strumilin, and Kritsman. Nevertheless, there is scope for a more detailed discussion of these processes within the context of the analysis provided by Grosskopf, particularly as Grosskopf relies more on Strumilin's stratification approach, rather than on that of Kritsman and his school, who were concerned to find 'direct indicators' of class.[3] There is still today a considerable amount of controversy over the mechanisms and extent of such class differentiation, as the works of Chayanov and Shanin already mentioned indicate. In addition, any critique of the state policy towards the countryside which is concerned with its effectiveness (or lack of it) in fostering socialist relations of production must include an analysis of the mechanisms and extent of development of capitalist relations of production.[4]

KRITSMAN'S WORK

To elucidate the processes of development of capitalist relations of production and a capitalist class structure, a substantial part of this article will be devoted to a discussion of the work of Kritsman, particularly of his *Class Stratification of the Soviet Countryside* [1926b]. Kritsman's work has recently been the object of renewed attention. For example, Shanin discusses his work as follows:

The main group of party scholars, led by Kritsman, developed research whose direction was governed by ideological commitment to detect a rising tide of polarisation. The hiring-out of horses and equipment was seen as the main new form of class-exploitation. It was predicted that socialism in the countryside would come as a result of state intervention and a rise in urban wages and productivity, which would rob richer farmers of their wage-labour and make their influence crumble. Few only defended the purity of the Marxist definition by which capitalist class-differentiation could be measured only qualitatively, ie. in terms of the predominance of wage-labour – which would have put it, in this period, next to nil [*Shanin, 1972: 60–1*].

Later, in discussing the methodological problems involved in the use of quantitative indices of wealth to analyse stratification, Shanin remarks:

The stratification by land sown was bitterly denounced by Kritsman and his lieutenants in the agrarian section of the Communist Academy. They claimed that this index was suitable only for the pre-capitalist period and that it helped to conceal real differentiation-processes because of the levelling of land-holdings which had taken place during the revolutionary period. Stratification of peasant households by capital and income was proposed as an alternative and put into operation in a Ts. S.U. [Central Statistical Administration – G.L.] handbook and in a study by Gaister, both published in 1928. This method revealed some new methodological weaknesses, however. The amount of land held was not taken into account, since it was not considered part of capital – a limitation which made estimates of actual production factors in terms of 'capital' doubtful. Moreover, any estimates of capital and income for peasant households in a type of economy producing a great part of its own needs were extremely dubious. In fact, the advantages of using indices of wealth and income in money terms were quite offset by the difficulties of correctly estimating them [*Shanin, 1972: 131–2*].[5]

However, despite various criticisms of Shanin's own position[6], interest in Kritsman's work as providing a possible alternative mode of analysis did not appear in Western publications until the work of Solomon [1975, 1977]. A comparatively favourable review by Harrison [1978b], however, suggests that Solomon is somewhat influenced by the multifactorial approach of Shanin. For this reason the more recent work by Cox [1979b] is of considerable interest, as is the 1979 article by Harrison. Cox [1979b] contrasts the positions of Shanin and Kritsman, and concludes his article by saying:

... furthermore, the Soviet research of the 1920s shows that Marxists have been able to deal with problems in the analysis of peasant society in a more flexible way which offers real insights into the complexities and peculiarities of the peasantry which neither Shanin nor the type of Marxism he attacks have been able to reveal.[7]

In his article in this issue Cox further develops his remarks on Kritsman and his colleagues, pointing to differences in interpretation among them, indicating the originality of Kritsman's own approach and defending him from some of Solomon's criticisms. Harrison, on the other hand, is somewhat more critical of the 'Agrarian Marxists', including Kritsman, but primarily on the grounds that they failed to transform their critique of the Chayanov school into a practical theory which would form the basis of the construction of an alternative, socialist mode of rural intervention [*Harrison, 1979: 95*].[8] In this way they constituted an early example of what Harrison calls 'subordinate Marxism', which tends to be restricted to an academic critique, rather than the presentation and practice of an alternative strategy.[9]

Yet it is not clear to me that Kritsman had no strategy for the socialist transformation of agriculture. He certainly had fairly well-developed ideas on cooperatives as a potential path to socialism, as well as of the conditions under which cooperatives could foster capitalist relations. For example, in an article entitled 'Ten Years on the Agrarian Front of the Proletarian Revolution' [1927a], he argued that rural cooperation was a field of fierce struggle between capitalist and socialist tendencies of development. Both forms of transformation of the petit-bourgeois economy depended on the self-activity of the small farms, and where capitalist elements did not predominate, this self-activity (collective, not individual) was a product of the interlocking of the petit-bourgeois economy and the state economy of the proletariat. This interlocking opened a way for the petit-bourgeois economy which was a non-capitalist road to the predominance of the petty economy, but not on the basis of its destruction, but of its organic development. Consequently, Kritsman was critical of the 1925 abolition of the direct formal prohibition (sustained for four years after the transition to the NEP) of capitalism in agriculture. This *de jure* recognition of what was already to a significant degree recognised *de facto* led among other things to the downfall of the hopes of the poor as a social stratum of retaining the means to raise up their own individual farm, because they did not dispose of enough of their own means of production to conduct their own farms. (Elsewhere Kritsman argued that the proletarian state should not create proletarians in the countryside.) In other words, Kritsman's view of a socialist strategy in the countryside was to provide the poor peasants with enough means of production to engage in petty farming in their own right, and to encourage various forms of cooperation: a conclusion remarkably similar to that of Grosskopf. In addition, as a means of combating Soviet bureaucratism, Kritsman advocated in this article the raising of the cultural level of wide strata, both ruling and ruled, and above all of the mass of the peasantry, and the attraction of large masses into social work and work of direction, to create the preconditions for the gradual liquidation of this 'survival of the past'. Superficially, at least, such a position is rather similar to that of Lenin and Bukharin as described by Harrison [1979: 96].[10] Kritsman's analysis of the mechanisms of class differentiation of the peasantry is thus related to a strategy for socialist development which was influenced by Lenin. It is also based on extensive knowledge of the research conducted not only by the

Chayanov ('Organisation and Production') School, but also the research conducted by his colleagues in the Agrarian Section of the Communist Academy, as well as research not identified with either school. It is precisely because his appraisal of the empirical material is related to a conception of forms of development of socialist relations of production that his work is so interesting.

Shanin is correct that part of Kritsman's strategy of socialist development involved the development of urban wage-labour to absorb rural unemployment (a change in the division of social production which would alter the social division of labour). However, as already indicated, he was more concerned with preventing the generation of that rural unemployment by developing socialist forms of organisation in the countryside, and by providing the means of production to poor peasants to sustain their farms until such times as they could enter or establish collective farms. Kritsman had reservations about the development of urban labour (at least in the short term) to absorb rural unemployment, because although urban employment was expanding, so was urban unemployment [*Kritsman*, 1925: 42–3]. Thus for Kritsman the mode of state intervention to encourage socialist relations could take a variety of forms, including the organisation of rural wage-labourers (*batraki*).

This approach to agrarian problems forms the background to Kritsman's investigations of the extent and forms of development of capitalist relations of production in the Soviet countryside of the 1920s. While such developments were important for a socialist strategy of transformation of the relations of production (one has to know the problem in order to solve it), Kritsman was careful not to overestimate the strength of rural capitalist development and to point to the social bases of socialist transformation (including the small but growing proportion of collective farms and state ownership of the commanding heights of the economy). This is particularly clear from *Class Stratification of the Soviet Countryside,* which is translated in a slightly condensed form in this issue.[11]

I have devoted a considerable amount of attention to one of Kritsman's works for a variety of reasons. Firstly, it is not widely available and provides an excellent account of the first half of the 1920s. Readers can readily decide for themselves how adequate my commentary is on Kritsman, but it seems fairly clear that a process of capitalist class differentiation was taking place, although it was in its early stages, as Kritsman emphasised. Given the debate still surrounding Kritsman's approach, the presentation of a detailed exposition seemed the best way to avoid misunderstandings as to the nature of his analysis. Secondly, Kritsman's work *Class Stratification of the Soviet Countryside* is exemplary in its painstaking attention to detail and its methodological sophistication. It is hardly a dogmatic approach; for example, he refused to argue by analogy (when faced with insufficient data in the two industrial *volosti*) that class stratification must be taking place. His grasp of the complexities of the changing division of labour and of regional diversity meant that he was unlikely to favour the use of any single index of class differentiation, and this probably formed one of the bases of his critiques even

of members of his own 'school'. Such critiques were not purely negative; they
were clearly made in order to improve later research – hence the preliminary
nature of his conclusions based on the empirical material presented. Thirdly,
Kritsman's work was related to both a historical analysis of the period and a
strategy which was similar to that of Lenin or Dzerzhinsky, and in some
respects to that of Bukharin. As Cox points out,[12] Kritsman had a conception
of structures within the Soviet social formation that was influenced by Lenin's
analysis in *The Tax in Kind* [*Lenin,* 1921], but Kritsman considered that
feudalism as a structure could be added to the five structures mentioned by
Lenin, especially for some parts of Central Asia.[13] This conception of
coexisting structures which interpenetrated each other was related to
Kritsman's view of the predominant role of the state sector in structuring the
economy. He argued that cooperation was a way of integrating the commodity
peasant farms into the general system of the Soviet national economy.

For this reason Kritsman placed great emphasis on the planning of
agriculture. This was surely the reason for his devastating critique of the Five
Year Plan produced by Kondrat'ev and Oganovskii for the *Narkomzem,* the
People's Commissariat of Agriculture.[14] Similarly, he placed emphasis on
particular policy measures which would help foster the socialist development
of the peasantry.

For example, he drew attention to the burden of taxation on the poor
peasants, and noted that it had been lifted. However, as Grosskopf points out,
in the absence of other policy measures, this adversely affected the marketing
of grain. Yet these 'absent' policy measures were of the kind also advocated by
Kritsman, or at least implied by his analysis.[15] (a) A credit policy favouring the
poor peasantry, which would enable them to buy means of production and thus
secure their independence of the prosperous peasantry (as well as providing
the preconditions for cooperative work, since there would be a basis for joint
purchase and use of such means of production). (b) A pricing policy on means
of production so that they were cheap for the poor peasantry (adequate indices
for the identification of poor peasants would have perhaps even made possible
a differential pricing policy which favoured the poor). As Grosskopf points
out, a policy of supplying implements at prices the poor could afford would
have encouraged them to deliver grain to market even in the absence of tax
pressure. Grosskopf, and following her Bettelheim, draws attention to the
economic conditions of such a policy of supplying cheap means of production
to the poor peasantry. It required the development of Department I industry,
and not only in the form of heavy industry or only in the towns. This implied a
diversion of resources away from what might be considered luxury consumer
goods for the towns, but it would have rapidly and cheaply led to increased
agricultural production, including production of industrial crops as raw
material for various industries, especially textiles. This was precisely what
Lenin intended by his advocacy of an alliance between heavy industry (metal
for agricultural implements) and the peasantry. It was a precondition for
developing cooperatives and collective farms on a voluntary basis, with
the incentive of rising living standards for the poor and middle peasantry.

(c) Finally, Kritsman's analysis of trading capital and his criticisms of the practices of trading cooperatives and mutual aid committees implied a policy of much more attention to these non-state forms of potentially socialist organisation. On this issue his views were similar to those expressed by Lenin in 'On Cooperation' [1923], but Kritsman was not simply following an official party line (which was in any case increasingly ignored): his views were clearly founded as much on the empirical material as on Lenin's remarks.

As Grosskopf demonstrates, the developing crisis of NEP, which finally came to be mistakenly considered in the party leadership as a 'grain strike' by the *kulaks,* was closely related to the failure to pursue such policies properly. Bettelheim [1978] provides additional grounds for adhering to such a view. Yet it is clear from Kritsman's analysis that the *kulaks* were often not a direct political danger; they were often in the Party and were beneficiaries of its policies in many unintended ways. Neither were they a serious economic danger, given the strength of the state sector, even if they were economically powerful in their own localities. Furthermore, the process of capitalist stratification had only just begun and could have been readily undercut by the sort of policies indicated above. One wonders how much attention was paid by the Party leadership to these studies, despite Kritsman's prominence.[16] It is doubtful if Stalin read the material (compiled by Central Committee members) presented on the Urals and Siberia before embarking on his 'Urals–Siberia' methods.

This is not to say that Stalin was unaware of the activities of Kritsman and the school of Agrarian Marxists. According to Solomon's account [1977: ch. 9], the first attack on Kritsman's analysis which both came from a Marxist and was coupled with a call for 'the congruence of research findings and Party dicta' had come from S. M. Dubrovskii.[17] By April 1929 the Agrarian Marxists were being accused of holding positions that conflicted with Party policy in the countryside.[18] By November 1929, the campaign to start immediate collectivisation of the peasantry had begun, and in December a Politburo commission was established to devise methods of implementing collectivisation. It was preparing to submit its proposals to the Politburo, just around the time when rural scholars were assembling in Moscow on 20 December 1929, for the start of the First All-Union Conference of Agrarian Marxists. While the Conference was to some extent remote from the political developments at the time, it is clear that the proceedings of the conference were being noted. For some reason, probably related to his earlier attacks on them, members of the Agrarian Marxist group launched an attack on Dubrovskii. Dubrovskii's reply centred on what he claimed was Kritsman's insensitivity to the heightening of class conflict in the period of transition to socialism. Solomon does not stress the point, but this was a departure from the lines of Dubrovskii's earlier attack on the Kritsman approach, where he had claimed that there were too many capitalists and poor peasants and too few middle peasants. The December 1929 reply by Dubrovskii thus appears to have been a *volte-face,* falling in line with Stalin's theoretical innovation of the time, the supposed exacerbation of class contradictions prior to their eradication with the completion of the transition to socialism.[19] It is therefore not completely surprising, with hindsight (although from Solomon's account, it electrified the Conference at the time), to discover that it was after Dubrovskii's defeat by Kritsman (on 27 December 1929) that Stalin appeared to address the delegates, and made his famous announcement that the *kulaks* were to be liquidated as a class.[20] The most immediate effect of this historic intervention was to neutralise the victory of the Kritsman school over Dubrovskii, and to prevent the development of what might be called an Agrarian Marxist establishment whose views did not fit in with the now predominant line on the countryside. Within months, the Agrarian Marxist school was being forced to leave the field of rural enquiry, a process which was completed early in 1932.

THE END OF NEP

Perhaps more than any other single event, Stalin's intervention in the Agrarian Marxist Conference signalled the end of the New Economic Policy, although for some time after it was claimed in some quarters that NEP was still being implemented. As indicated earlier, there is still debate today over whether NEP was compatible with a programme of industrialisation; this is usually taken to mean that NEP implied a policy of concessions to the *kulaks,* forced on the Soviet state by the reaction of the peasantry to the compulsory requisitions of War Communism. Such a view of NEP is common in Western historiography, as Grosskopf points out,[21] but she argues convincingly against the view that the Soviet regime had a tragic destiny to coerce the peasantry into a socialist orientation. Such an approach, she argues, is heavily influenced by the 1925 ideology, associated with Bukharin, which was a response to the fact that the government had practically neglected the poor peasantry during the years 1923 to 1925 [*Grosskopf,* 1976: 286].

This neglect of the poor peasantry was exacerbated by the 'Provisional Ordinances' promulgated in the spring of 1925, which decisively accelerated the differentiation of the peasantry [*Grosskopf,* 1976: 316–19]. In the spring of 1925 there was a grave shortage of agricultural implements, since there had been virtually no process of replacement of implements since the beginning of the First World War, and they had worn out. The 'Provisional Ordinances' were designed to reduce the great disproportion between the extent of land and the few instruments of production possessed by the majority of the peasants, which was retarding the optimal development of agricultural productivity. However, this was attempted by repealing the agrarian code of 1922, whose objective had been to protect the disadvantaged peasants against exploitation from the *kulaks.* (It will be remembered that Kritsman protested against this precisely because of its effect on poor peasants.) According to the source cited by Grosskopf, this removed restrictions on the employment of poor peasants as wage-labourers. It was above all the large individual farms of the most important cereal regions (North Caucasus, Urals, Siberia, the Crimea) which profited from this possibility. *Rabkrin* (The Workers' and Peasants'

Inspection) showed in 1927 that in these areas, 75 per cent of wage-labourers were working on average 13 hours per day. Thus the 'Provisional Ordinances' reinforced the dependence of poor peasants on the *kulaks,* a development which is sometimes treated as the enlargement of NEP (or 'neo-NEP'). This policy amounted to a provisional abandoning of the passage to a socialist agriculture, as the Party leaders of both right and left acknowledged [*Grosskopf,* 1976: 317].[22] It was precisely in 1925 that the terms of credit for the poor peasants deteriorated, so that implements were not delivered to them until too late, after the autumn. The result was the situation which Lenin had warned against in 1920: it became difficult to supply the towns with food. The failure of the Soviet government to provide the qualitative social conditions to assure commodity production by agriculture led to the grain crisis of 1925. It was above all the poor peasantry which refused to sell its harvest (the fiscal pressure to do so had also been relaxed).

Far from this being a *kulak* grain strike, as Kamenev supposed, it was a policy failure by the Soviet government. Instead of the government making its planned 70 per cent of all its grain purchases by 1 January 1926, it had scarcely more than half the grain it needed by then. The figures on which Kamenev based his view of a '*kulak* grain strike' (a theme later taken over by Stalin) were challenged by a government commission.[23] The decisive mistake, however, had been that Kamenev had confused the indications of the Central Statistical Administration on the distribution of grain surplus with those on the distribution of marketed grain. Even peasants with little or no surplus in fact sold part of their harvest, although they had later to buy back, at a greater price, the grain necessary to feed themselves. Thus, although Grosskopf does not put it this way, Kamenev's confusion is related to a form of agricultural planning which was mistakenly restricted to working on net surpluses from agriculture. Because of this, calculations tended to be based on an overall balance of supplies between agriculture and industry, which ignored the conditions of existence of different types of peasant enterprise and hence class relations. (This mistake is also evident in the 1924 *Narkomzem* plan, judging by Kritsman's comments.) The result of this mistake in Kamenev's case was the illusion that only the *kulak* supplied produce to feed towns or raw material for industry. The poor peasants had few means of getting the money to pay the former tax in kind (which had been changed in 1924 to a money tax). In the most important grain regions, the possibility of getting money for non-agricultural pursuits was greatly reduced [*Grosskopf,* 1976: 142]. Yet the poor peasants normally bore the brunt of the agricultural tax. The poor and middle peasants also bought the majority of urban manufactured products, rather than the rich peasants, as Kamenev claimed.

Kamenev claimed in 1925 not only that the rich peasants were most involved in commodity exchange, but that the cooperatives mostly helped the rich peasants [*Grosskopf,* 1976: 169]. Certainly Kritsman's work provides some evidence that this was so, but he also pointed to the genuinely cooperative use of the means of production, a point which is further reinforced by Grosskopf. Grosskopf argues that the willingness of the poor peasants to engage in the *supryaga* (collective use of means of production and, even in her view, of credits) and other forms of spontaneous mutual aid was responsible for an increase in the proportion of middle peasants by 1926–7, compared to 1924–5. The result of this was to lead to a specific feature of rural class differentiation in the later 1920s. The growth in the numbers of the rural proletariat was not at the expense of the middle peasantry, but as a result of the decomposition of the class of poor peasants: while one part of the poor peasants completely lost its economic independence, because of the difficulties just described, and enlarged the ranks of the rural proletariat, another part succeeded in integrating with the class of middle peasants, the number of which continued to increase throughout NEP. According to Grosskopf, this evidence confirmed certain Party claims on the pattern of rural class differentiation.[24] This development suggests very strongly that while capitalist relations were developing fairly rapidly in the countryside, particularly after the 'Provisional Ordinances' of 1925, the option of undercutting this development by a policy of support for the poor peasantry still remained. Such a policy would have generated a much greater marketing of agricultural produce than the *kulaks* could manage on their own.

Such a policy, however, was more difficult to pursue after 1925. From 1925 onwards agricultural productivity declined because of the price policy of the Soviet government which meant that the poor peasants lost hope of escaping from their misery by their own efforts, and their dependence on the *kulaks* became habitual. This reduction in productivity took place despite the fact that at this point agricultural technical equipment began again to be made available. When the Soviet leadership provisionally renounced the pursuit of the road to socialism in the rural sector, they deprived themselves of an important means of increasing cereal production, according to Grosskopf [1976: 319]. This corroborates the view expressed by Kritsman, and while there is undoubtedly some truth in it (the political conditions of economic performance are often neglected), the reduction in productivity may have been partly due to the weather and to remaining equipment wearing out even faster than it was replaced.

The effects of this approach to agriculture became evident by the winter of 1927–8. Despite the fact that when the 1927–8 plan was definitively fixed in August 1927, it was estimated that the grain harvest would be 2.5 per cent down on the previous year,[25] the plan envisaged an increase in grain deliveries of 11 per cent (and an increase in the agricultural surplus of 14.1 per cent) over the previous year. The months October to December were essential to the campaign of collecting grain, since at that time both the demand by the national economy and the supply of grain were at their maximum. The cereal crisis of 1925–6 had shown that the factors determining the supply of grain from October to December were mostly subject to Soviet power and could be methodically regulated. The policy on grain collection during 1926–7 showed that the government had accepted this: the agricultural tax had been reimposed, a lot of industrial commodities had arrived in the grain surplus regions from October to December 1926 and the costs of collecting grain had been reduced considerably (making it possible to reduce the gap between state and private prices, and between autumn and spring prices, at least outside the villages). Consequently, marketed grain reached a new record [*Grosskopf,* 1976: 329]. This made the state policy during 1927–8 all the more remarkable. Sufficient grain stocks were not built up during the summer of 1927. Manufactured goods which could have been sold in grain surplus regions were diverted to urban markets, because of the so-called 'goods famine' again, which resulted from increased wages in state industry in the summer of 1927.[26] On top of this, to celebrate the tenth anniversary of the Revolution, the poor peasantry had received a dispensation from the payment of almost all the agricultural tax and the taxes on the other sections of the peasantry had not been raised. With a reduction in taxes and the absence of a stock of commodities to exchange against cereals, the mistake of the autumn of 1925 had been repeated. Rich peasants had sold significantly during the summer of 1927, prior to the anticipated price reduction in October, but from October to December, the supply of grain had greatly diminished. Far from being a *kulak* grain strike, this was a 'strike' by the poor and middle peasants, exacerbated by the passive attitude of the state and cooperative collecting organs [*Grosskopf,* 1976: 333]. This passive attitude was partly the result of poor preparation and contradictory orders from the state, which wished to prevent competition between purchasing agencies from undermining the state price policy, although the control figures of Gosplan indicated that no such competition was likely and Gosplan was insisting that the buyers pursue an active policy of encouraging peasants to market their products.

Yet the grain collection results were not particularly bad after the end of December 1927. They only appeared bad in the light of the annual economic plan mentioned above, and in relation to the XV Party Congress held in December 1927 which discussed the implementation of the first Five Year Plan. In 1925–6 the Soviet government had been able (after the autumn crisis) to improve grain purchases considerably, so that eventually the growth in the agricultural marketed surplus for that year surpassed the increase in gross production. At least one of the devices used earlier was still available in January 1928: an increase in agricultural prices was rightly rejected because, as before, it would have led to grain speculation the following year. However, an increase in prices in certain regions, coupled with an increase in deliveries of commodities would have been economically and politically effective. This was because what were usually grain surplus areas had a relatively poor harvest in 1927, whereas areas in the industrial centre, for example, had a more successful harvest. On top of this, state purchase prices, which had been 27 per cent above cost prices in 1925–6, were only 1 per cent above cost prices in 1926–7, and 0.4 per cent above in 1927–8. An increase in price, coupled with a greater supply of commodities, in the relatively successful areas would almost certainly have yielded bigger state purchases. Instead, from January to July 1928 (with a short break in April) 'extraordinary measures' were taken, under the direction of Stalin, who toured the regions normally considered as grain surplus areas, plus Siberia [*Grosskopf,* 1976: 334–6]. (Hence the 'extraordinary measures' were sometimes referred to as the 'Urals–Siberia' methods, before the rest of the Party came to appreciate the significance of the phrase.)

The result was that in the spring of 1928, peasants in the normal grain surplus areas unexpectedly repurchased grain on the open market (as opposed to the intra-village market). For all regions, the open market purchases by peasants exceeded those of the previous year by 40 per cent. This caused unexpected difficulties for the distribution of the grain surplus, with the overall result that, far from increasing by 14.1 per cent over the previous year, as envisaged in the plan, it diminished by 18.5 per cent. Thus the pace of industrialisation seemed threatened, both in terms of grain exports and supplies to the towns. Hence the cereal crisis of the summer of 1928 was the result, not of a *kulak* grain strike, but of the 'extraordinary measures' themselves. As Grosskopf puts it [1976: 343], it became clear at this point, precisely because of the exigencies of a methodical and accelerated industrialisation, that the rules of NEP had to be strictly followed. These rules were, firstly, that agriculture should not supply its products beyond its own capacity, or peasant repurchases would increase further, and secondly, that the Soviet state should not suppress private commerce before it was able to replace it. Grosskopf follows this with a critique of Stalin's famous article 'On the Grain Front' which used Nemchinov's data to claim that small-scale peasant production was incapable of supporting industrialisation. Grosskopf argues that thanks to the technical alliance between industry and agriculture, and the social alliance between the working class and the poor and middle peasantry, such a strategy would have been possible. However, the technical alliance advocated by Lenin had not been implemented: in 1926–7 the instruments of production in agriculture had reached at most 60 per cent of their 1913 level (and this, rather than peasant consumption, as claimed by Stalin, was the main cause of the restriction of agricultural deliveries to the towns). Similarly, the 1925–6 crisis had shown how fragile the social alliance was. Nor had cooperatives been seriously promoted by 1926–7. Thus the principal tasks of NEP as outlined by Lenin had scarcely been undertaken by 1926–7.

As is well known, the grain crisis of 1928 (prompted by the 'extraordinary measures' which contradicted the Party line established at the XV Party Congress and which were conducted without the knowledge of much of the Party leadership) produced a wider crisis in NEP. The reaction of the peasants to these measures was the same as to the grain requisition of the Civil War – to sow less. This then appeared to justify to a wider section of the party the use of 'extraordinary measures' and to gain support for the idea of a sharpening of class conflict in the transition to socialism, as well as for the idea of rapid collectivisation of the peasantry. The use of 'extraordinary measures' was repeated on a larger scale in 1929, and, as was mentioned in the discussion of Kritsman, by December 1929 a Politburo Commission was established to devise methods of implementing collectivisation. These developments were tragic, but also ironic in view of the fact that the technical, political and organisational preconditions of collectivisation had been virtually neglected during NEP. The technical conditions were the supplying by industry of the instruments of production to raise the level of equipment above the 1913 level. The political conditions were to ensure that this equipment was distributed to the poor and middle peasants, and the organisational conditions were the encouragement of cooperatives as a means of achieving the transition to a socialised agriculture. Grosskopf's evidence indicates that in the later 1920s such developments were happening to some extent anyway, despite the neglect of most of the Party leadership, and that where they occurred, they were having the expected effect of encouraging both the marketing of grain and the development of collective forms of agriculture. Furthermore, contrary to Stalin's suggestion that peasant consumption was a potential threat to industrialisation, Grosskopf shows that urban consumption was a greater threat since it adversely affected exports by 1927 in comparison with 1913 [1976: 351]. While the intensification of agriculture had taken place during the 1920s, particularly in oil-seed and vegetable crops, rather than grain, it was still the case that in 1928–9, between 25 and 30 per cent of the 1913 sown area in the former 'granary' area was still fallow. Grain production was still 10 per cent less per capita than before the First World War, although production of other foodstuffs such as milk and meat had surpassed the 1913 level [*Grosskopf*, 1976: 349]. Thus the grain figures were misleading if one took them on their own, ignoring the changing structure of agricultural production. Nevertheless, there was still a great potential to increase grain production in the fallow areas by supplying more means of production. The effect of the 'extraordinary measures' was to reduce the amount of livestock, which meant less meat and milk, and greater difficulty in ploughing. While Stalin was in a sense correct that grain was marketed less than before the First World War, this was offset by the production and marketing of other agricultural products which were important for the national economy. The growth in urban consumption between 1926 and 1927 was entirely at the expense of exports.

On the evidence provided by Grosskopf, it is clear that Western (and to some extent, as she says, Soviet)[27] historiography was wrong to take its analysis of the 'need' for collectivisation from Stalin's analysis of small-scale peasant consumptionist farming being incapable of supplying the raw material for industry and the food for the towns and for export. Far from the NEP policy being played out economically, it had in important respects not been given a proper chance in agriculture. A policy of supplying further means of production, quite apart from aiding a further intensification of agricultural production, would have facilitated a growth of grain production by recultivating the fallow land in the pre-war 'granary' area.

CONCLUSION

One must conclude that the demise of NEP was largely a result of its faulty implementation. The dangers of an incorrect method of implementing NEP were signalled as early as the 'Scissors Crisis' of 1923, but they should have been clear enough by the time of the cereal crisis of 1925, when the restoration of the economy to pre-war levels was virtually complete. As Grosskopf points out, Dzerzhinsky clearly analysed the general lines NEP should take prior to his death in 1926. During 1926–7, the Soviet government implemented its agrarian policy in a manner which suggested it had learned the lessons of the previous year. The change of course in the following year seems primarily to be related to the struggle going on in the Party leadership at the time. The XV Party Congress had not been a clear victory for Stalin, and this appears to be related to his clandestine use of 'extraordinary measures' against the peasantry, mobilising the support of that section of the party which had always seen NEP as a retreat and who were only too ready to believe that Kamenev's mythical '*kulak* grain strike' had again become a reality in the autumn of 1927.

Clearly in this situation, the emphasis of the Agrarian Marxists, and particularly of Kritsman, on the careful evaluation of the mechanisms of class differentiation, its extent and its implications for the construction of economic plans, was completely vindicated. While the Kritsman school were not the only ones to supply important evidence on the state of agrarian class relations in the 1920s and to attempt to relate it to economic policy, they were just reaching the point of sufficient pre-eminence in the field to have a real potential for influencing Party policy in favour of continuing NEP *as a means* of industrialising the economy and collectivising the peasantry, when Stalin intervened so dramatically to neutralise them as a potential political force. It will never be known how the Agrarian Marxist school would have developed, but their careful work clearly has implications for current policy in some developing countries. They were interested in the agrarian class structure not just as a matter of academic curiosity, but as a vitally important component of a rural (and urban) development strategy. Precisely because the class structure affects the capacities of various economic agents, it has a considerable impact on the effectiveness of state policy.

NOTES

1.   Smith had access to the typescript of Tribe and Hussain before it was published. Barsov's approach is not universally accepted: see the critique by D. Morrison [1982].

2.   It is perhaps worth stressing that the apparent vindication in Grosskopf of Lenin's position on the peasantry as it was developing towards the end of his life, cannot be dismissed simply on the grounds that Grosskopf is the latest in a long line of Marxists suffering from an uncritical adulation of Lenin. There may be some force to such a criticism of Bettelheim's analysis, however. See, for example, the review of the first volume of Bettelheim's work [1976] by R. Miliband [1975]. Yet whatever force there is to such an argument against the 'apotheosis' of Lenin, Miliband pushes it too far. While Miliband's remarks on 'Economism' and the 'State Bourgeoisie' are quite acceptable, the review deteriorates in the section entitled 'From Leninism to Stalinism'. While the first volume of *Class Struggles . . .* does concentrate too much on Lenin, it does treat Lenin's changes of position seriously, and more importantly,

contrary to what Miliband suggests, it does not treat the development from Leninism to Stalinism as a single evolving process rather than clearly marking the break between the two. It is difficult to see how the first volume could be read in such a way, and the appearance of the second volume even more clearly undermines such an interpretation of Bettelheim's position. The second volume is clearly concerned with analysing the break between Leninism and Stalinism. Bettelheim's critical view of Stalinism is perhaps made clearer in C. Bettelheim and B. Chavance [1981]. Whatever one may think of its argument, it clearly treats Stalinism as a *transformation* of Bolshevism produced by the class struggles of the late 1920s to the 1950s.

3. See Cox's article in this issue.

4. Feudal or pastoral nomadic relations will only receive passing treatment here, since their impact on the development of socialist relations was of secondary importance during the 1920s.

5. Shanin [1972: 211] also quotes Kritsman's reference to the peasantry as a 'petit-bourgeois mass'.

6. See, for example, G. Littlejohn [1973a] and the ensuing debate: Shanin [1973] and Littlejohn [1973b]. See also M. Harrison [1977a].

7. The discussion of Kritsman here could be considered complementary to that of Cox.

8. Harrison evidently depends heavily on Solomon [1977] for this judgement.

9. Harrison argues that later critiques of Chayanov or of other general conceptions of 'Peasant Economy' suffer from similar limitations. He specifically refers to three articles, namely M. Harrison [1977b] and J. Ennew, P. Hirst and K. Tribe [1977]. The third article is G. Littlejohn [1977]. Certainly at the time of writing my critique of Chayanov I was in no position to suggest socialist modes of intervention among the peasantry, and I was well aware of the fact. It had already been made painfully clear to me, even at the time of writing my earlier critique of Shanin, that I could not even successfully grow a dozen lettuces. However, Harrison is correct in attempting to analyse the problems of the lacuna of any 'negative' theoretical critique: it does indeed provide no strategic or tactical political guide, and this is a serious limitation.

10. While I accept that Bukharin was attempting to defend and elaborate the ideas which Lenin developed towards the end of his life, I have pointed to certain theoretical and political weaknesses in Bukharin's position in G. Littlejohn [1979]. See also K. Smith [1979].
    It is also clear from the already cited remarks by Grosskopf on Dzerzhinsky that Bukharin was not alone in his attempt to defend the line advocated by Lenin. Indeed, it is at least arguable that Trotsky and Preobrazhensky were also attempting to do so, although their interpretation was clearly different from that of Bukharin or Dzerzhinsky. What is of interest here is that Kritsman also shows a considerable degree of familiarity with Lenin at various points in his work. There is evidence that this was publicly recognised, since in 1925 Kritsman gave a paper entitled 'Lenin and the Road to Socialism' to the Communist Academy on the first anniversary of Lenin's death [*Kritsman*, 1925e]. In the light of this, it is somewhat surprising to find Solomon arguing that in their eagerness to discredit their former teachers (the Chayanov school) 'the members of the agrarian section of the Communist Academy had neglected to discuss the role of cooperatives. Given the commitment of the Communist Party after 1926 to increasing the importance of these institutions, this neglect left the Agrarian Marxists open to criticism' [*Solomon, 1975*].

11. See particularly the beginning of *Class Stratification*, where Kritsman counselled against both complacency and panic in dealing with the question of the extent of capitalist relations. Such advice could not have been more well placed, yet it was effectively ignored, with complacency the order of the day until about 1925 (particularly on the part of Bukharin), and panic in at least a section of the Bolshevik leadership with the developing crisis in the NEP from the winter of 1927–8. While Kritsman's work did show that capitalist relations were

becoming stronger, he finished *Class Stratification* by reminding the reader of processes in the countryside favourable to a socialist strategy: see the end of the translation.

12. T. Cox in Part I, pp. 54–5.

13. It is also possible to add 'pastoral' relations of production with reference to the Buryat Mongols in the Soviet Union, although the impact of both the Romanov state and in Mongolia itself the impact of the Manchu dynasty was to make the relations of production feudal in certain respects. See Caroline Humphrey [1974, 1978: 133–60, 1979]. The complexity of such relations of production raises questions as to the usefulness of conceptualising the articulation of these relations as an articulation of structures, as Cox does; the danger being that one may fall into implying that the essences of each structure are co-present in the social formation. Preobrazhensky [1926] seems to me to fall into this position: see G. Littlejohn [1979].

14. The plan was called 'Osnovy Perspektivnogo Plana Razvitia Sel'skogo i Lesnogo Khozyaistva', published in 1924, and edited by Teodorovich. Kritsman's critique [1925h] was given to the Praesidium of Gosplan in 1925, and was called The Plan of Agriculture and Industrialisation. (See the Appendix to this article.)

15. For further discussion of these issues, see G. Littlejohn [1984] *A Sociology of the Soviet Union,* London and Basingstoke: Macmillan, especially Chapter Two, 'Hammer and Sickle: Problems of a Worker-Alliance'.

16. See M. Lewin [1968: 71–8] for a discussion of the controversy over the definition of the *kulak,* including the views of Kritsman and his colleagues. Only in June 1929 did the *Sovnarkom* accept the hiring out of equipment as a criterion for including a farm in the *kulak* category (ibid., page 74). Lewin also describes the controversy over stratification and the reception of Kritsman's work in Chapter 2 (ibid., especially p. 47). However, although he is right that the significance of the indices of stratification varies, by not explicitly setting these variations in the context of an analysis of the division of labour (and of geographical variations in it) Lewin seems to undervalue the usefulness of Kritsman's work. Lewin was right to argue (page 49): 'For the moment, the difficulties of studying the stratification of the peasantry proved insurmountable, and in the end no valid and authoritative survey of this intractable problem was ever produced.' However, it is surely evident from Lewin's account that this was partly because of the political debate which forced some of Kritsman's colleagues, such as Gaister, to retract their results. The studies were not authoritative in the sense of being accepted, but despite their problems they were surely authoritative in terms of their level of analysis. Gaister was apparently forced to retract his results because they were being used by the Left Opposition to support its own arguments.

17. Solomon [1977] had the chance to interview Dubrovskii on a bi-weekly basis in 1969 (ibid., page 188). This attack in January 1928 had little effect at the time.

18. There is no suggestion that Dubrovskii made this charge at this point [*Solomon, 1977: 162*].

19. As Harrison points out in his 1978 review of Solomon, she provides no account of Stalinism, which Harrison rightly argues should not be treated as having an impact on academic life from outside. The attack on Kritsman by Dubrovskii can surely only be understood as giving voice within the academic agrarian debate to the views of the ascendant Stalinist sections of the party. However, such a conclusion is based purely on the theoretical similarities between Dubrovskii's remarks and the ascendant Stalinist line on the countryside. Solomon, by not drawing attention to these similarities, seems to corroborate a remark made by Cox in Part I (pp. 53–4): 'The problem with her interpretation, both on this specific question and on the work of the Agrarian Marxists in general, is that in attempting to locate the research in its social and political context she tends to lose sight of the theoretical basis of the research which provides the logic of the categories chosen.' Paradoxically, in the case of the December 1929 attack on Kritsman by Dubrovskii, losing sight of the apparent theoretical basis of the remarks makes it somewhat more difficult to locate them in their political

context. The similarities of Dubrovskii's remarks and the position of the Stalinist sections of the party are fairly evident, and this suggests that there may have been some substance to Kritsman's charge, in reply, that Dubrovskii was an opportunist [*Solomon,* 1977: 167]. In my view Solomon is completely misleading in treating Kritsman and Dubrovskii as showing an almost equal lack of intellectual honesty and restraint. Dubrovskii had indeed taken Kritsman out of context, as the latter claimed.

20. Stalin began his speech with the denunciation of five 'bourgeois' prejudices which he claimed were rampant in current rural enquiry, including those of the Chayanov school. In my critique of Chayanov [*Littlejohn,* 1977] I give the impression in a footnote that Chayanov was the main opponent of the Marxist approach to the peasantry, and that this was why Stalin attacked him. It is clear from Solomon's account, which despite certain disagreements I found very interesting and informative, that the criticisms of 'bourgeois' prejudices were merely a prelude to the core of the speech. Chayanov's school had in many respects already lost the argument to the Agrarian Marxists, and the speech, particularly its famous announcement on the liquidation of the *kulaks* as a class, rendered the entire Agrarian Marxist Conference irrelevant.

21. S. Grosskopf [1976: 283–4] draws particular attention to Lewin's exposition of such a position: see M. Lewin [1968: 133–5]. However, on page 317 she does not forget to point out the similarities in the work of E. H. Carr [1970].

22. Grosskopf quotes both Rykov and Trotsky to this effect. Thus it is not only Western historiography which has shared the view that agricultural investment required concessions to the *kulaks;* in effect, the entire Party leadership took this view. Its corollary is, of course, that the *kulaks* were an obstacle to industrial investment.

23. Grosskopf [1976: 140]: it was a *Rabkrin* commission, directed by Yakovlev, Tsyl'ko, Rybinkov and Chelintsev, and its members included Paskovskii, Lositskii, Lifshits, Vishnyevskii, Groman and Strumlin. The definition of the social categories of peasants in the evidence available to Kamenev was on the basis of sown area, which the commission criticised. (Thus Kritsman was by no means alone in his scepticism about the use of sown area as an index of class relations.) The results of this survey were published in extracts in *Pravda* in December 1925 and republished in a 100-page brochure in 1926 [*Yakovlev,* 1926]. It is difficult to see how the Party leadership could have been unaware of this.

24. Grosskopf [1976: 311]: in a footnote, she argues that this contradicts the supposition of Lewin [1968: 56–7] that such a pattern of class differentiation only existed in the proclamations of the Party. It seems to me that Grosskopf's evidence should not simply be taken at face value, however. Kritsman's emphasis on the diversity of forms of cooperation, and the diversity of effects of this in terms of class relations, is probably correct. While Grosskopf's evidence is more systematic and apparently convincing than that of Lewin, Kritsman's remarks on what could be reported as 'spryaga' or 'supryaga' (mutual aid) makes one a little wary of the evidence supplied by Grosskopf. The same is true of her evidence on page 312 of the growth of 'simple' production cooperatives during NEP.
    Yet it must not be forgotten that in the late 1920s Kritsman was also emphasising the growing spontaneous movement into cooperatives and collectives. Furthermore, Grosskopf's case against Lewin on this point is supported by two further points which she makes elsewhere in her book. Firstly, on page 396, she refutes the suggestion of Carr and Davies [1969: 117] that during NEP the process of redivision of farms was extended to the middle and poor peasants. This refutation is on the basis of evidence provided by Khryashcheva. Many of the redistributions were fictional to avoid tax on large-scale enterprises. If this is the case, then one of the grounds disappears for Lewin's doubts about the supposedly 'special nature of differentiation' at this time. Lewin claims [1968: 57] that if the numbers of *serednyaks* (middle peasants) were not decreasing, it was because they were being reinforced by frequent divisions of households, whose members, while formally continuing to be classified as *serednyaks,* were becoming poorer as a result of these divisions.

Grosskopf argues that repartitions were only about two to three per cent of all farms, and that these were more numerous among the prosperous than the middle peasants. This argument, if accepted, certainly undercuts the grounds for Lewin's doubts about the 'special nature of differentiation'. The second point which Grosskopf makes (which strengthens her case on the role of cooperatives in supporting some of the poor peasantry) is the evidence and argument on pages 415–19 which shows the growth in cooperatives for soil improvement, use of agricultural machinery, improvement of seeds and livestock breeding and rearing. None of this was reported under the heading of *supryaga* so the doubts raised by Kritsman about some forms of *supryaga* do not apply to these cooperatives.

According to Solomon [1977: Chapter 6] the Agrarian Marxists themselves found that the middle peasant refused to disappear. This may appear to support Grosskopf's claim that the middle peasantry was not disappearing. However, Grosskopf relies heavily on the conceptions of Strumilin, as well as the evidence of Khryashcheva, for her conclusions. Kritsman's work should not be identified with that of either of the latter two researchers. Solomon's reference to the 'middle peasant' in describing the work of the Agrarian Marxists is misleading if it is taken to refer to an independent peasantry standing outside of relations of exploitation between households. Rather, the Kritsman group were arguing that differentiation had not yet radically altered the basic character of the peasantry as small commodity producers (neither capitalist nor proletarian, in the majority of cases, even though enmeshed in the processes which were producing class differentiation). This difference between the position of the Agrarian Marxists and the approach of, say, Strumilin, on whom Grosskopf relies at this point, does not adversely affect the overall argument presented by Grosskopf, nor the implicit similarity between Grosskopf and Kritsman in their approach to economic policy towards the peasantry.

25. Grosskopf [1976: 327]: a few months later it became clear that the harvest was in fact 6 per cent less than the previous year.

26. C. Bettelheim [1978] dwells on this point at length: see Part III, on the contradictions and class struggles in the industrial and urban sectors. N. Lampert [1979: Chapter 2] also provides evidence on some of the tensions within the industrial sector in the 1920s, which suggests that attempts were made to bolster up the authority of the technical intelligentsia in order to help restore Soviet industry. It is possible that wage increases to the workers were an attempt to contain the resentment generated by this strengthening of managerial authority. Whatever the causes of the wage increases, they fostered the diversion of manufactured goods away from the countryside, which did not help the *Smychka* between workers and peasants.

27. See, for example, Part I, Chapter 1 of Yu. V. Arutyunyan [1971]. There one can find arguments that in the 1920s peasant commodity production was not sufficiently mobilised for the needs of industrialisation, because of the poor price relations for the peasantry, called forth by the backwardness of *light industry* (pp. 23–4, my emphasis). On page 28 we find the claim that the peasantry applied its means of production irrationally, and on page 31 we find a discussion of agrarian overpopulation. All of these arguments ignore the basic *lack* of means of production of the peasantry, and in effect blame the peasantry for the failure of NEP. The remark on the irrational use of means of production is reminiscent of Stalin's claim to Churchill that the peasantry were reluctant to use tractors and other machinery. Grosskopf shows that this was not the case in the 1920s [1976: 248–50].

Appendix: The Plan of Agriculture and Industrialisation

It was mentioned in the main text of this article that Kritsman provided a devastating critique of the plan produced by Kondratiev and Oganovskii, for *Narkomzem*. This issue is briefly discussed by Jasny [1972: 167–72] in my view without indicating how penetrating Kritsman's critique was. Part of the reason for Kritsman's interest in the *minutiae* of the collection of agricultural statistics was because of their potential for plan construction and policy formation, a potential that was very real because of the extensive apparatus for collecting statistics developed after the Revolution. Grosskopf [1976] argues that there was a lack of relation between the collection of statistics and plan construction between 1917 and 1921. It is evident from Kritsman's critique of this 1924 Five Year Plan of *Narkomzem* that these problems had not been fully overcome.

According to Solomon [1977: 19], Kritsman, the Marxist historian who would become the leader of the Agrarian Marxist group, was in 1925 a lone voice who challenged the planners' view that agriculture would continue to be conducted by a large decentralised mass of individual farms. He was apparently silenced with the assertion that socio-economic change in the countryside was out of tune with the Party line in the rural sector. Solomon also points out that this plan has not received much attention from Western historians, apart from E. H. Carr. For these reasons, it is perhaps worth giving a brief account of Kritsman's criticisms of this plan.

Kritsman argued that the principles of the plan were either commonplace or wrong [*Kritsman*, 1925h reprinted in 1929c]. It was a platitude for an economic plan to envisage the development of the productive forces. The other principle of the plan, namely a two-sided agrarian-industrial development, similar to the United States, was either a general phrase or was wrong. Kritsman argued against the idea of an undefined 'Narodnik-mystical' harmony of agriculture and industry, but he was also against industrialisation at the expense of agriculture. The facts showed that the Soviet Union was not developing agriculture in proportion to industry. In the last two years, agriculture had been growing at 4 per cent per annum, as against 30–40 per cent for industry, so that agriculture after the famine was at the same level as in 1920.

Kritsman then distinguished between 'projection' plans and plans of 'current' production, arguing in 1925 that it was only possible at that time to plan 'current' production for one year ahead. (He added in a 1929 footnote that in the changed situation one could plan further ahead.) The use of an extrapolation or 'projection' type of plan showed that agriculture could not be much influenced at that time from the outside, but if that were accepted, then Kritsman argued that one should go in for *short-term* extrapolation. A five-

year extrapolation was unfulfillable; a five-year plan was only possible when
one could regulate what was planned. He showed that even within a year, the
differences between the plan and the actual figures were huge. The
extrapolations had been poor; they were mostly too pessimistic, and this may
have undermined the confidence of the Agricultural section of Gosplan. The
perspective plan had failed brilliantly (that is because it was so overfulfilled,
with various branches achieving between 50 and 90 per cent of the five-year
target in one year). This did not occur accidentally. One should not approach
the charting of a perspective plan for agriculture by individual branches, as this
plan sought to do. For such an approach to be realistic, it was necessary to
narrow the limits of the plan (to one year). Otherwise the plan had to be
constructed in another way. A detailed calculation of the market, of the
possibilities of selling, and of the possibilities of production, was necessary.
This meant one had to take account of the class structure of the peasantry, or at
least recognise that it was difficult to plan where class differentiation was not
what was assumed in the plan. Kritsman argued that such a calculation was not
taken into account in the plan. The plan talked of the peasantry in general, not
of its division into groups, and then mentioned as a general phrase: 'The
process of socio-economic differentiation of the countryside . . . in its turn is a
factor . . . the significance of which must be taken into account.'[1]

Yet Kritsman did not overstress this differentiation, arguing that it was less
in the countryside than in the towns. He argued that in each branch of
agriculture it was necessary to separate the commodity side from the
consumption side. To do so it was necessary to take account of the interesting
data on how the *batrak* (rural wage-labour) was paid wages. This varied in
different regions. There were not enough data on this, but without an
apportionment of the commodity-producing groups of the peasantry in market
areas, it was easy to arrive at erroneous conclusions. Consequently, it was
necessary, first, to classify branches (of agriculture) into market and non-
market areas, and, second, in the market areas themselves to separate
commodity and non-commodity farms. Related to the latter were the (in
essence) proletarian part of the peasantry, on the one hand, which worked a
certain plot of land with alien means of production, and on the other hand,
partly related to this were some groups of peasants who were independently
running their own farm, in so far as they did not produce for the market.
Without such an analysis (which was fraught with difficulty, of course) the
serious elaboration of a perspective plan for agriculture was impossible.

It was also insufficient to give definite figures for an agricultural (as for an
industrial) plan: one ought to give plan variants and say how it would work in
relation to other plans. Not only was this plan unsatisfactory from the point of
view of the resolution of the problems posed (which among other things was
showed by a comparison of the plan and its realisation), it was also
distinguished by its quite exceptional slovenliness, and by the rather strange
(to say no more) character of the work. Despite the published criticisms of
various faults, the *Narkomzem* did not try to correct the plan. It had fallen to
Kritsman to show the various statistical and arithmetical errors, primarily in

the work of Professor Oganovskii. A special commission had been set up in *Narkomzem,* which confirmed everything shown by Kritsman, but was limited to these points. Then Professor Kondrat'ev appeared in print with the observation that Kritsman's charges against him were unsubstantiated. Kritsman had then showed that his charges in relation to Kondrat'ev were more than sufficiently substantiated. Following this a list of printers' errors were published. Kritsman then pointed out various other problems with the plan, such as its claim that between 1921 and 1923 the number of working horses had increased by 5.1 per cent, whereas in a footnote Professor Lositskii said that the number of working horses went down by six per cent in 1922, giving an overall reduction in the number of horses by 1923. Such inconsistencies were even acknowledged in the main text of the plan. Kritsman took the view that a plan completed in this manner could not serve as a basis for judgement. The plan could not calculate the resources of the peasantry, nor the resources of the state, since its compilers were mistaken on both counts.

The plan had only been fulfilled in a bureaucratic sense. The calculation of Professor Makarov showed that the plan was not implemented; the conclusions of the agricultural section (of Gosplan) on each point showed that the plan was not implemented. It could not be implemented. By the whole of its construction, the perspective plan for the development of agriculture presented a strange combination of a Marxist and non-Marxist approach to the matter. The latter approach had been correctly characterised in the journal *Bolshevik* as a 'turn of the century' approach,[2] and it was visible in many parts of the works of *Zemplan*. This was evident in their treatment of the Soviet Union as an example of state capitalism, which was like private capitalism, only regulated by state power, an approach which contrasted with Lenin's. Furthermore, the growth of the national population was taken as one of the bases for the construction of the plan. Kritsman argued that this amounted to the theory of rural overpopulation as the basis for the growth in productive possibilities, due to the quantity of working hands, quite contrary to the views of Marx on the relative decline of the agricultural population. The attempt to base agricultural development on population growth meant in practice a huge army of unemployed, the basic solution to which was the growth in industry. On the supply side, there was no need in current conditions to fear a lack of workers. If one approached the matter of population growth from the demand side, then the growth in population played a different role for the two main parts of agriculture: for that part of agriculture which supplied the means of production (that is, raw materials for industry) and for that part which supplied the means of consumption (that is, food products). If one proceeded from the point of view of the market for food products, then of course the growth of population played a colossal role. But it would be laughable on the basis of changes in the population of the USSR to seek to form the extent of the market for foodstuffs. This would require an examination of the dependence of foreign markets on foodstuffs produced in the USSR.

In conclusion it was necessary to say that the perspective plan bore a quite strange character, combining an attempt at a communist, Marxist approach with an approach of a quite different sort which appeared in many places, in conclusions and in the posing of questions. It was right to return this work to the *Narkomzem* and to propose that it be reworked in a radical manner, both in its principles and its execution. Here as in other cases, it was necessary to say what was the state of affairs, and thus to achieve the correction of what was done badly.

It should be clear from the brief account of Kritsman's criticisms of this plan that he was not so much advocating 'socio-economic change' as Solomon puts it (although he definitely favoured the growth of cooperatives as a way of transforming agriculture) but was criticising the theoretical assumptions of the plan, as well as the shoddy workmanship which was evident in its construction. It should also be clear that his interest in the various processes of differentiation of the peasantry was related to his interest in plan construction: adequate plans for both developing agricultural production and developing socialist relations in the countryside (and town) had to take account of the changing class relations, including the development of commodity production, and their impact on the markets for agricultural products.

NOTES

1. See especially the 'Preamble' and Chapter One, Section III.
2. This was a euphemism for a Narodnik approach.

III. Class Stratification of the Soviet Countryside*

L. N. Kritsman

The development of capitalism in the countryside gives no basis for panic because large-scale industry in the hands of the proletariat is now [*1926*] growing more quickly than rural capitalism, and at the same time the dependence of all agriculture, including its capitalist part, on state large-scale industry, transport, wholesale trade and credit is growing. The development of capitalism in the countryside is taking place at the same time as the fall in the share of agricultural capital in the general production of the country. The development of rural capitalism is not a serious threat, but neither does it provide grounds for complacency. The way to avoid both complacency and panic is to study the countryside, groping around for those specific forms of approach (methods of study) which correspond to the specific peculiarities of the process of class stratification of the peasantry in the Soviet countryside – only after such work has been done will it be possible actually to study the process itself. Otherwise one would just be piling up useless data. For this reason I have concentrated in this work on the elaboration of data which does not cover the majority of regions, but is detailed. One must draw a distinction between the 'dynamics' and 'statics'[1] of 'class stratification'.[2] To say that a farm 'is becoming' capitalist is not to say how far that process of 'becoming' has gone. The process of class stratification in the Soviet countryside is only beginning and it is hoped that this work will help to clarify the question. In brief, then, the concentration upon detailed studies in this work is to help develop methods of research. This requires both a discussion of the historically specific context of the stratification and a critique of the 'banal' approach to these issues, to be found in much of our statistical literature.

The specific result of the anti-feudal revolution (in the countryside) was the growth in the mass of independent small-scale farms not employing wage-labour, that is the economic rise of the middle peasantry, transforming the feudal or semi-feudal organisation of peasant agriculture. This was the economic root of the union of the proletariat and middle peasantry, strengthened after the Revolution by the NEP legalising the commodity form of connection between the state economy of the proletariat and the small farms (as well as among the small farms themselves, of course). This was the form demanded by the interests of the farming peasantry and of small farms in general. Previously well-to-do

Translator's Note: This work has been edited and condensed, as well as translated, to make it more accessible to the contemporary reader. I have numbered all tables, provided comments or summaries of various points in italics, and provided a series of translator's notes giving further comments where it seemed better not to include them in italicised form in the text. With regard to Russian measurements, one desyatin = 1.09 hectares = 2.7 acres; one pud = 16.38 kilograms. – G.L.

peasants were compelled to let poor peasants use their stock and livestock free of charge; the transition to the NEP, however, signified the eradication of this right. This led to the transformation of the potential of the capitalist strata of the peasantry and the deterioration among the poor of their own farming. Nevertheless, the process of class stratification is relatively slow.

In studying this process, one must caution against the use of 'direct' indices of the development of rural capitalism, such as the juridical renting of land or the hiring of wage-labour. This is because of historical circumstances, including the illegality of some of these relations which means that they are partly hidden, and because we are dealing with the early stages of the process of class stratification following the Civil War. (*Elsewhere Kritsman referred to Lenin's remarks on the inappropriateness of using wage-labour as an indicator of the presence of small-scale rural capitalism, so wage-labour was not played down because it was next to nil, nor was there any 'purity' of a Marxist definition of capitalist relations in terms of wage labour to be defended.*)[3] One can define the weak and the poor farms as those whose labour power cannot be fully used on their own farm: in other words, for whom there are insufficient means of production. The prosperous (or well-to-do) farms are those whose means of production cannot be fully used by means of their own labour power: in other words, for whom there is insufficient labour power. Thus in its initial stages the process of class stratification appears as the strengthening of differences in the power (capacity) of farms.

The need to study the process of class stratification on the basis of groupings of peasant farms according to indirect indices (the extent of the farms) makes the 'banal' approach to the resolution of the problem particularly dangerous. The material on the dynamics of stratification is not large and is quite ill-assorted. All these materials suffer from mistakes both in the primary sources and in their approach to the matter (methodology) not to mention mistakes in calculation. As an example of the mistakes in the primary sources, one can cite an article by Vishnevsky [1925] which uses some data from the *Altaiskii Ezhegodnik* for 1922/1923:

TABLE 1

SOWN AREA FOR ONE FARM ACCORDING TO:

Sown area groups	Dynamic studies	Short budget studies	Excess according to short budget studies
	desyatins		
Without sown area	—	0.98	0.98
Up to 0.5 *des.*	0.34	0.72	0.38
0.6– 1.0 *des.*	0.85	1.41	0.56
1.1– 2.0 *des.*	1.53	2.35	0.82
2.1– 3.0 *des.*	2.49	3.78	1.29
3.1– 4.0 *des.*	3.56	4.68	1.12
4.1– 6.0 *des.*	5.02	6.11	1.09
6.1– 8.0 *des.*	6.69	7.34	0.65
8.1–10.0 *des.*	9.59	12.0	2.41
10.1–16.0 *des.*	12.52	15.75	3.23

The farms which according to the dynamic studies have no sown area, have (according to the more reliable data of the short budget studies of the same farms at the same time) a sown area of on *average* around one *desyatin,* and the range of error for other groups is evident from the right-hand column.

The entirely relative character of groupings by sown area makes particularly dangerous its routine introduction into the explanation of the process of class stratification of the countryside. Under such circumstances, a judgement as to the stratification or equalisation of the peasantry is made only according to the growth or decline in the percentage of the extreme sown area groups, which in any case does not coincide with the extreme class groups of the peasantry (capitalistically exploited and exploiting). Only a comparison of different kinds of data on the different groups of the peasantry can give sufficient material for judgement on the process of stratification of the peasantry.[4]

Consequently, although studies of individual villages, *volosti* and regions are particularly 'sinful' in their approach to the matter, they contain much more detailed data which make it possible to call into question their economic analysis. In addition, because of the small extent of the region and of the groupings themselves (in particular, grouping by sown area), they bear a much less abstract character because of the unified trend of agriculture (the interrelation of different branches of agriculture) within the limits of a small region. The analysis of data on individual villages, *volosti* and regions gives – besides the immediate results – the chance to judge the adequacy of less detailed data on bigger territorial units (*gubernii* and so on) for the explanation of the process of rural class stratification.

One can conclude this critique of the routine (or banal) approach by an analysis of data from six rural Soviets (*sel 'sovety*) in the Bogaevskii and Semikarakorskii regions of the Don area, which shows the interrelation between sown area and working livestock in 1924. The figures covered 3573 farms, and were taken from a brochure entitled *The Face of the Don Countryside* [*Litso* . . . 1925]. The grouping by sown area gives the following results:

TABLE 2

Farms	Percentage of all farms	Percentage of sown area
Without sown area	15.4	—
Up to 1 *des.*	23.1	4
1– 2 *des.*	15.5	7
2– 4 *des.*	19.3	19
4– 6 *des.*	11.8	19
6–10 *des.*	9.6	25
10–16 *des.*	3.8	16
16–25 *des.*	1.3	8
Over 25 *des.*	0.2	2
	100.0	100

These figures show that while 54 per cent of farms disposed of only 11 per cent of sown area, less than 15 per cent of farms disposed 51 per cent of sown area. Yet while they reveal deep differences between groups of peasants distinguished by the extent of their farms, the figures do not show the interrelations between the different groups of peasants. It would be quite mistaken to group peasant farms on the basis of sown area into poor, middle and prosperous. The grouping by working livestock tells more of the relations of different groups of the peasantry:

TABLE 3

Farms	Percentage of all farms	Percentage of working livestock
Without working livestock	70.2	—
With 1 head	9.8	13
With 2 head	13.7	37
With 3 head	3.3	14
With 4 head and more	3.0	36
	100.0	100

This table shows that half the working livestock was in the hands of 24 per cent of the farms, and the other half was in the hands of six per cent of the farms. Regrouping the two distributions into three groups with the large-scale farms owning half of all working livestock (or sown area), the smaller owning the other half, and the third group consisting of farms owning no sown area or working livestock, one can present the following comparison:

TABLE 4

PERCENTAGE OF FARMS

	Large-scale	Smaller	Possessing none	Total
Grouping by working livestock	6	24	70	100
Grouping by sown area	15	70	15	100

This table shows that the 70 per cent of farms devoid of the basic means of production – working livestock – could not for this reason be actually independent farms, but were the objects of exploitation. The exploiting farms were hidden among the remaining 30 per cent, in all probability, among the higher group classified by working livestock. But only the comparison of both groupings, that is, by the farm and by the extent of its own means of production, uncovers the picture of the interrelations of the different groups of the peasantry. (*But to establish these relations more clearly it was necessary for Kritsman to examine the technical division of labour.*) The brochure indicates that the 'loading' on one animal was four *desyatins*, that is, that one animal was necessary to cultivate this area. The loading differed in each type of farm, depending on its agricultural stock (implements), the quality of its working livestock and so on. It was less in a small-scale and greater in a large-scale farm (where one horse could provide the basis for the cultivation of a greater area). For this reason the establishment of a general norm of loading conceals the actual extent of stratification. Nevertheless, using this norm gives the following grouping:

TABLE 5

	Percentage of all farms	Percentage working livestock	The average for 1 farm of head of working livestock
Without working livestock or sown area	15	—	—
Without working livestock and with sown area	55	—	—
With insufficient working livestock	4	8	1.6
With sufficient working livestock	16	39	1.8
With a surplus of working livestock	10	53	4.0
	100	100	

If one wished to subdivide the highest 10 per cent of farms, then three per cent disposed of more than 36 per cent of the working livestock, averaging 8.9 head of livestock per farm. Relating this to sown area produces the following table (which excludes farms with no sown area):

TABLE 6

Among farms	Percentage of all sown area
Without working livestock and with sown area	36
With insufficient working livestock	14
With sufficient working livestock	32
With a surplus of working livestock	18
	100

Thus the 10 per cent of farms with a surplus of working livestock officially concentrated in their hands only 18 per cent of all sown area, but actually (assuming those with insufficient livestock used half of their own land, that is, seven per cent of all sown area) the farms with 'excess' livestock concentrated no less than 61 per cent of all sown area in their hands. Relating this to Table 5, this same 10 per cent of farms disposed of 53 per cent of working livestock and held in dependence on themselves 74 per cent of the farms. Only 16 per cent of farms, disposing of 39 per cent of the working livestock and 32 per cent of the sown area, could be considered as independent farms, neither exploiting nor exploited, ignoring the possibility that some of these could be hiring wage-labour.

Comparing the results of the grouping by sown area and by working livestock, one finds that of the 15 per cent of the farms in the highest sown area grouping, six per cent had insufficient working livestock, around six per cent had sufficient working livestock and around three per cent had 'excess' livestock. Of the 51 per cent of sown area which this 15 per cent of highest sown area farms disposed of, more than 20 per cent belonged to farms with insufficient working livestock, 18 per cent to farms with sufficient working livestock and only 12 per cent to farms with 'excess' working livestock.

In other words, using the technical norm of the 'loading' on livestock as an index for calculating access to the means of production, Kritsman was able to establish that the grouping by sown area did not coincide with the class grouping of the peasantry. He was similarly able to establish a discrepancy between the grouping by working livestock and his class grouping of the peasantry, but it was not so great as that between sown area and class. Despite the apparent power of this critique of the use of sown area as an index of class differentiation, Kritsman was very careful to point out the limitations of his alternative approach as a means of analysing the class structure. The full details of these qualifications cannot be reproduced here, but they show that Kritsman understood that the above analysis did not apply to the whole of the USSR, and that among other things he understood the importance of organisational forms of the unit of production – that is, of the technical division of labour – for class analysis.

Briefly, Kritsman indicated that a part of those with no sown area could be petit-bourgeois or even capitalists in other branches of the economy than agriculture. In addition, some of those without working livestock could be petit-bourgeois or even capitalists, in so far as they were not engaged in agriculture but in market gardening or viticulture (vine-growing), each of which was developed in one of the six sel'sovety *being investigated (although a horse was still necessary to them as means of transport). Some of the biggest farms would be hiring working livestock but not as exploited farms. Finally some (but not many) of the farms with insufficient working livestock might be using tractors. Furthermore the grouping introduced above defined farms only by the comparison of the extent of their sown area and the extent of their working livestock, employing a general norm of a loading on one head of livestock. This concealed class stratification because it did not reflect exploitation on the basis of the hiring of stock, or the open exploitation on the basis of hiring day workers or time-rate workers. Having thus made this critique of the 'banal' approach and established the need to use as many indices as possible, taking account of the specific situation in different parts of the country, Kritsman was in a position to examine the few detailed studies then available which contained pertinent information.*

He began with studies of individual villages. He knew of only one investigation containing serious material, which covered seven villages and five auly. *It had been conducted by a commission of the South East Bureau of the Central Committee of the Russian Communist Party. The results were published in 1924, and it will be referred to here as the South East Study* [Yancheskii, 1924]. *This was followed by a study of individual* volosti. *To illustrate the relation of these* volosti *to the overall economy, the map overleaf shows the* gubernii *in which most of the* volosti *and villages analysed by Kritsman are to be found. (The map is taken from p. 71 of Grosskopf [1976] and indicates the proportion of non-peasant private property in the total cultivated surface of Russia in 1916. This in itself provides a useful pre-revolutionary reference point for the developments in the first half of the 1920s analysed by Kritsman.)*[5] *The map provides a rough indication of the extent of capitalist development before the Revolution in various* gubernii *(or provinces, as Grosskopf calls them). Unfortunately, it only covers European Russia.*[6]

The material that was used by Kritsman, then, is as follows:

A.   *The South East Study. This consists of villages in the Don and Kuban regions of the Stavropol Gubernia and the Georgian Republic.*

B.   *The Agricultural Centre:*
    (i)   *The Nikol'skaya Volost' in Kursk Gubernia*
    (ii) *The Znamenskaya Volost' and the Pavlodarskaya Volost', both in the Tambov Gubernia.*

C.   *The Transvolga:*
The Malotolkaevskaya Volost' in the Samara Gubernia.

D.   *The Ukraine:*
The Shamraevskaya Volost' in the Kiev Gubernia.

E.   *The Industrial Centre and the North West:*
    (i)   *The Yaropolskaya Volost' in the Moscow Gubernia.*
    (ii)   *The Tsurikovskaya Volost' in the Smolensk Gubernia.*
    (iii) *The Goritskaya Volost' in the Tver Gubernia.*
    (iv)   *The Prokshinskaya Volost' in the Pskov Gubernia.*

F.   *The Urals:*
The Petrovskaya Volost' in the Bashkir Republic
This refers to data from three former volosti *which were combined into one, and from several villages of the Chelyabinsk and Perm areas.*

G.   *Siberia and Kazakhstan:*
    (i)   *The Shchuch'inskaya Volost' in the Akmolinskov Gubernia.*
    (ii)   *The Alexandrovskaya Volost' in the Kustanai Gubernia.*
    (iii) *The Tisul'skii Region of the Tomsk Gubernia.*

The Urals, Siberia and Kazakhstan are not shown on the map presented by Grosskopf.

PROPORTION OF NON-PEASANT PRIVATE PROPERTY IN THE TOTAL
CULTIVATED SURFACE IN RUSSIA IN 1916

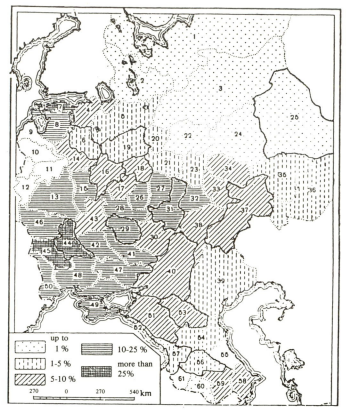

PROVINCES

1. Arkhangelsk	16. Smolensk	31. Tambov	46. Volhynia
2. Olonets	17. Kaluga	32. Penza	47. Ekaterinoslav
3. Vologda	18. Moscow	33. Simbirsk	48. Kherson
4. Petrograd	19. Tver	34. Kazan	49. Taurida
5. Novgorod	20. Yaroslavl	35. Ufa	50. Bessarabia
6. Pskov	21. Vladimir	36. Orenburg	51. Kuban
7. Estonia	22. Kostroma	37. Samara	52. Black Sea
8. Livonia	23. Nizhegorod	38. Saratov	53. Stavropol
9. Kurland	24. Vyatka	39. Astrakhan	54. Ter
10. Kovno	25. Perm	40. Don	55. Dagestan
11. Vilna	26. Tula	41. Kharkov	56. Tiflis
12. Grodno	27. Ryazan	42. Poltava	57. Kutai
13. Minsk	28. Orel'	43. Chernigov	58. Baku
14. Vitebsk	29. Kursk	44. Kiev	59. Elizavetopol
15. Mogilev	30. Voronezh	45. Podolia	60. Yerevan
			61. Kar

A. THE SOUTH EAST STUDY

*Although this study covered only 12 villages (*aul *being the kind of village found in the Caucasus and Central Asia), Kritsman devoted a considerable amount of space to their analysis, on the already mentioned principle that examination of detailed studies could provide the basis for the evaluation of studies of larger territorial units.*

The biggest failing of the research is the arbitrary selection of reported data. For example, for some villages the data report only sown area groupings, in others grouping by working livestock, and so on. Yet the data are quite interesting and relatively detailed. They show a decline in sown area between 1917 and 1922, followed by a rise in 1923 to about half the 1917 sown area. The research report claims that the contemporary *kulak* is different from the pre-revolutionary *kulak* in trying not to distinguish himself from the peasant mass. Exploitation is often hidden in the form of the *spryaga* (*a form of apparently communal use of implements sometimes called* supryaga) or 'nephew's service', and sown area registered as belonging to the poor in fact partly includes sown area belonging to *kulaks* (for tax evasion purposes). Grouping by sown area gives the following picture:[7]

TABLE 7

STARO-MAR'EVSKII VILLAGE: PERCENTAGE OF FARMS

	Without sown area	Up to 2 *des.*	2–4 *des.*	4–10 *des.*	10–16 *des.*	Over 16 *des.*	Total
1917	8.8	3.8	12.8	28.0	24.6	22.0	100.0
1920	1.3	7.0	27.0	55.0	8.5	1.1	100.0
1922	3.1	20.4	37.3	38.1	1.1	0.1	100.1
1923	7.0	13.1	2.7	44.3	11.3	1.6	100.0

Thus from 1920–2 there was a so-called 'movement downwards' and from 1922–3 an almost pure 'movement upwards' but from 1920–3 there was undoubtedly differentiation by sown area.

TABLE 8

GIAGIISKII STATION:[8] PERCENTAGE OF FARMS

	Without sown area	Up to 1 *des.*	1–2 *des.*	2–4 *des.*	4–6 *des.*	6–8 *des.*	8–10 *des.*	10–13 *des.*	13–16 *des.*	Over 16 *des.*	Total
1917	38.2	2.6	3.6	8.8	13.7	7.2	7.7	5.1	5.1	8.0	100
1920	25.1	8.4	8.5	20.6	12.1	9.8	6.2	5.3	2.0	2.0	100
1921	16.2	11.4	10.6	25.9	11.4	6.8	8.1	5.1	2.6	1.9	100
1922	15.6	5.6	9.3	24.1	18.8	11.7	7.1	4.6	2.0	1.1	100
1923	15.7	5.9	9.4	19.8	19.6	12.8	6.8	5.5	2.7	1.8	100

TABLE 9

DYACHKINO SETTLEMENT: PERCENTAGE OF FARMS

	Up to 1 *des.*	1–4 *des.*	4–10 *des.*	10–19 *des.*	Over 19 *des.*	Total
1917	27.6	12.2	28.0	16.8	15.4	100
1920	13.6	21.4	47.4	13.7	3.9	100
1921	15.4	49.4	30.9	2.4	1.9	100
1922	24.0	26.8	33.9	11.5	3.8	100
1923	13.0	24.5	29.3	23.1	10.1	100

In Staro-Mar'evskii the extreme groups grew only in the latter period. In Giagiiskii Station the same was true, although the growth in the lowest groups was completely insignificant. In Dyachkino Settlement, there was a growth only of the highest groups, evidently because farms without sown area were not distinguished from those with up to one *desyatin*. There are no quantitative data on sown area for other villages, so one must proceed to data on the provision of working livestock used by each farm when the farms were grouped by sown area:

TABLE 10

STARO-MAR'EVSKII VILLAGE: LIVESTOCK PER FARM

	Without sown area	Up to 2 *des.*	2–4 *des.*	4–10 *des.*	10–16 *des.*	Over 16 *des.*
1917	1	0.35	0.5	1.6	3	4.25
1920	—	0.27	1.03	2.22	3.65	4.1
1922	0.4	0.25	0.8	1.4	3.1	4
1923	0.07	0.08	0.36	1.9	2	2.8

The general fall in livestock did not hit the highest groups so hard (those with over four *desyatins* of sown area). A similar pattern is evident for Dyachkino Settlement:

TABLE 11

DYACHKINO SETTLEMENT: LIVESTOCK PER FARM

	Up to 1 *des.*	1–4 *des.*	4–10 *des.*	10–19 *des.*	Over 19 *des.*
1917	0.12	0.73	2.24	3.64	6
1920	—	0.69	2.23	2.92	5.33
1922	0.3	0.99	1.36	1.73	3.42
1924	—	0.11	0.95	1.53	3.74

This difference in the provision of working livestock weighed most heavily on the lowest strata of the countryside, in that the number of farms without livestock grew:

TABLE 12

PERCENTAGE OF FARMS WITHOUT WORKING LIVESTOCK

	Dyachkino Settlement	Kievskii Village	Bystryanskii Khutor
1915	—	—	11.0
1917	—	15.8	13.8
1920	—	—	53.9
1921	28	—	50.3
1922	36	—	52.1
1923	—	43.4	52.7
1924	37.5	—	—

In Bystryanskii Khutor, the farms without working livestock were almost entirely those with up to four *desyatins,* and by 1923 they also included 42 per cent of those with between four and ten *desyatins.* A similar pattern is evident in the growth of farms without stock (instruments of production); in Bystryanskii Khutor 23.8 per cent of farms had no stock in 1917, 38.5 per cent in 1922 and 41.8 per cent in 1923. As with livestock, these farms were almost entirely those with up to four *desyatins,* but also included around 40 per cent of farms between four and 10 *desyatins.* While such evidence might suggest that (*at least in the South East*) sown area was a reasonable index of class differentiation in the early 1920s, it was only possible to decide this on the basis of data on stock and livestock. What is most clear from this is the extent of class differentiation, and it is supported by other evidence. The researchers claimed that the hiring of stock and livestock from the prosperous farms was growing all the time in Giagiiskii Station. This sometimes occurred under the cover of 'neighbourly work' or *spryaga.* In Bystryanskii Khutor the percentage of farms engaged in the *spryaga* was as follows:

TABLE 13

BYSTRYANSKII KHUTOR: PERCENTAGE OF FARMS WITH A SOWN AREA

Up to 1 *des.*	1–4 *des.*	4–10 *des.*	10–19 *des.*	Over 19 *des.*
92.3	87.4	69.8	92.7	100.0

The middle farms engaged in the *spryaga* least, and when they did so, according to the researchers, they did so with other middle farms, so that it bore a cooperative character, and could form the basis for collective peasant agriculture. The lowest farms did so with the highest farms, when it amounted to a form of exploitation (a form of hiring of wage-labour).[9] There was also a growth of rural wage-labour – for example, among the roughly 200 households of the Dyachkino Settlement, there were 65 *batraki* in 1917, five in 1920, seven in 1922 and 29 in 1924. According to the researchers, this was probably an underestimate, since it was hidden by both those hiring and by the *batraki* themselves. In addition, work was paid for by the day but there was no fixed limit to the working day, which meant it was a quite oppressive form of employment.

The prosperous farms also ruled on the grain market as the following table indicates:

TABLE 14

PURCHASES AND SALES OF GRAIN: DYACHKINO SETTLEMENT

	Farms selling grain*	Grain sold per farm	Farms buying grain*	Grain bought per farm
Up to 1 *des.*	—	—	27	24
1– 4 *des.*	22	31	22	12
4–10 *des.*	48	41	24	20
10–19 *des.*	63	78	31	11
Over 19 *des.*	100	141	25	102

percentages within each sown area grouping.

Thus none of the farms in the lowest group sold grain, but more than a quarter of them bought it. Furthermore, the percentage selling grain increased in the groups with a larger sown area, while the percentage buying fell on the whole among these highest groups. The purpose of buying among these higher sown area groups was in any case the resale of grain later, as the following table shows:

TABLE 15

BYSTRYANSKII KHUTOR: PERCENTAGE OF GRAIN SOLD AT DIFFERENT TIMES OF THE YEAR

Farms	In August–September	In October–November	In December–February	Total
Up to 1 *des.*	—	—	—	100
1– 4 *des.*	74	8	—	82*
4–10 *des.*	24	43	33	100
10–19 *des.*	8	25	66	100
Over 19 *des.*	3	15	82	100

there is evidently a mistake in this grouping, but it does not affect the overall relationship. Probably 18 per cent was sold in December–February.

The farms with up to four *desyatins* sold about three-quarters of their grain at the end of the summer at low prices; the farms with over 19 *desyatins* sold four-fifths of their grain in the spring at higher prices. The prosperous also gained more benefits from cooperation:

TABLE 16

DYACHKINO SETTLEMENT

	Number of farms	Members of cooperative	Percentage in cooperative
Up to 1 *des.*	27	2	7
1– 4 *des.*	51	8	16
4–10 *des.*	61	20	33
10–19 *des.*	48	14	29
Over 19 *des.*	21	9	43

This refers to a consumer cooperative with a membership fee of five roubles, and could be compared with the figures provided by Yakovlev in the brochure 'Our Countryside' [*Yakovlev, 1924*].

TABLE 17

PERCENTAGE OF FARMS

	Up to 1 *des.*	1–4 *des.*	4–10 *des.*	10–19 *des.*	Over 19 *des.*	Total
Among members of cooperatives	4	15	38	26	17	100
Among non-members	16	28	26	22	8	100

The only contrary evidence in the South East Study was a remark that the poor predominated in a cooperative with a membership fee of one rouble 50 kopecks, but no data were provided. The overall picture is sustained by the access of the prosperous to credit cooperatives:

TABLE 18

DYACHKINO SETTLEMENT

	Number of farms	Members of credit cooperative	Percentage in credit cooperative	Number receiving credit	Percentage receiving credit	Roubles per farm receiving credit
Up to 1 *des.*	27	1	4	—	—	—
1– 4 *des.*	51	24	47	—	—	—
4–10 *des.*	61	26	43	8	13	74
10–19 *des.*	48	32	67	11	23	87
Over 19 *des.*	21	18	86	3	14	100

According to the researchers, the same farms were receiving credit who were exploiting the poor by means of the *spryaga* and 'working off' (as a form of repayment). The poor in the credit cooperative received no credit, but seven cases were recorded of credit being given to the poor by the *kulaks*. There was a similar situation in Bystryanskii Khutor:

TABLE 19

BYSTRYANSKII KHUTOR

	Number of members of credit cooperative	Number receiving credit	Roubles per farm receiving credit
Up to 1 *des.*	—	—	—
1– 4 *des.*	13	—	—
4–10 *des.*	15	5	100
10–19 *des.*	15	5	88
Over 19 *des.*	3	1	50

The prosperous farms also paid relatively less agricultural tax. In Vinodel'ny the rate of tax per *desyatin* of sown area was as follows:

TABLE 20

VINODEL'NY VILLAGE: AGRICULTURAL TAX

Farms of sown area	Roubles per farm
Up to 2 *des.*	5.2
2– 4 *des.*	5.6
4–10 *des.*	12.1
10–16 *des.*	14.5
Over 16 *des.*	11.6

Thus farms with a greater sown area paid less tax per *desyatin*, partly because they obtained reductions due to a better knowledge of the law and better farm management. Even the Committee of Mutual Aid ran enterprises which were profitable for the prosperous, effectively making it a committee of 'self-supply'.

The data on the Georgian countryside are quite scanty. The researchers have claimed that there was a growth of the middle type of peasantry, but this was on the basis of provision of land. They also provided the following table, showing that differentiation was beginning again in 1923. (*It should be borne in mind that there was famine in 1921 in the USSR.*)

TABLE 21

WORKING LIVESTOCK IN GEORGIA; PERCENTAGE OF FARMS

	Without working livestock	With 1 head	With 2 head	With 3 head	With 4 head	Total
1920	17.3	47.9	26.4	5.5	2.9	100
1922	27.9	49.3	19.4	2.8	0.6	100
1923	19.1	44.9	27.4	6.3	2.3	100

The percentage of farms without sown area in Georgia were 1920 – 5.8, 1922 – 6.5, 1923 – 3.1, so the number of (presumably dependent) farms grew, that is, those with a sown area but no working livestock.

One can conclude this analysis (*of the South East Study*) by saying that despite the partial and somewhat chaotic nature of the data, there is no doubt that a process of (class) stratification of the peasantry is taking place, with the lowest groups in terms of sown area being transformed by their dependence on the highest groups, so that they are working with alien means of production, and with the growth of rural wage-labour, although its extent is not clear. (*I have reproduced this part of Kritsman's analysis at some length both because it is a good example of how to rework rather poor data and because it gives an idea of the sort of processes taking place at village level.*)

B. THE AGRICULTURAL CENTRE

(i) Nikol'skaya Volost', Kursk Gubernia
These figures are much more systematic than the above study and all refer to the same subject of research – the *volost'*. Yet they are much less detailed, and do not include the farms which were liquidated between 1917 and 1922. This undersampling is quite significant for 1917 and less so for 1922. The following table compares the survey by Yakovlev published in 1923 with the results of the agricultural census:

TABLE 22

	Farms		Population		Sown area	
	Survey	Census	Survey	Census	Survey	Census
1917	100	100	100	100	100	100
1920	119	101	103	98	119	89
1922	126	101	109	95	120	94

(*Kritsman also discussed the undersampling in terms of absolute figures and proposed to compare both sets of figures where possible.*) The survey gives the following distribution of farms by sown area:

TABLE 23

PERCENTAGE OF FARMS

	Without sown area	Up to 1 des.	1–2 des.	2–4 des.	4–8 des.	8–13 des.	Over 13 des.	Total	n
1917	16.5	12.5	18	23.5	20	7.5	2	100	612
1920	5	6	14	39.5	32	3	0.5	100	730
1922	4	7	15.5	42	29	2.5	—	100	775

Thus the middle groupings by sown area grew. Such a result is usually taken to mean that a process of equalisation rather than stratification is taking place. (*A similar result appeared in a grouping by (official) land-holding.*) However, the distribution by working livestock gives a somewhat different impression:

TABLE 24

	Without working livestock	With 1 head	With 2 head	With 3 head	With 4 head	With 5 head and more	Total
1917	24	36	26	9.5	2.5	2	100
1920	19.5	57.5	18.5	4	0.5	0	100
1922	22.5	64	12.5	1	0	0	100

However, the actual meaning of these tables is clear only if one compares them with each other (the figures in brackets are those from the agricultural census):

TABLE 25

PERCENTAGE OF FARMS

	Without land	Without sown area	Without working livestock	Excess of farms without working livestock over farms without sown area	Hiring horses
1917	6	17 (10)	24 (18)	7 (8)	8
1920	0.6	5	19.5	14.5	15
1922	0.4	4	22.5	18.5	26

While there was a steady decline in the proportion of farms without land or sown area, after 1920 there was an increase in the percentage of farms without working livestock. In addition there was a steady increase in the percentage of farms hiring horses. The number of farms hiring horses is directly proportional to the excess of farms without working livestock over farms without sown area, so the hiring of horses is clearly a direct economic necessity for those farms with a sown area but no livestock. Not only horseless farms hire horses, as can be seen from the 1922 figures. Often they are hired by one-horse farms because of some misfortune, such as the horse being ill. The main conclusion to draw from this data is that in 1917 farms without livestock did not sow, that is, did not conduct their farming, but in 1920 and especially in 1922, they did conduct their farm with alien working livestock. The acuteness of the change between 1917 and 1920 shows that this process of hidden transition of farms to an essentially proletarian state took place to a significant degree during 'War Communism'. It is impossible to forget that simultaneously with the growth in such hidden forms of capitalist exploitation went the decline in open forms, so that with the transition to the NEP the extent of capitalist exploitation was not very great. It is possible to estimate this by the number of farms without working livestock. The transformation of more small farms into capitalist ones doubtless took place in connection with the lowering (economically) of those very farms possessing means of production. With the sharpening of competition, this phenomenon will doubtless begin to disappear. The farms with a small sown area are predominant in hiring horses:

TABLE 26

PERCENTAGE OF FARMS WITHIN EACH SOWN AREA GROUPING WHO HIRED HORSES
(1922)

Without sown area	Up to 1 *des.*	1–2 *des.*	2–4 *des.*	4–10 *des.*	Over 10 *des.*
20	58	33	19	12	—

This picture is confirmed by the data on stock, the other main means of production:

TABLE 27

NUMBER OF FARMS

	Without stock	Excess of those without stock over those without sown area	Renting ploughs, sokhi* and harrows
1917	168	67	34
1920	168	132	94
1922	172	141	118

*(sokhi *are a kind of wooden plough.*)

Again the hiring of implements is proportional to the excess of farms without stock over farms without sown area, so the hiring of stock was evidently necessary for those farms with a sown area but no implements. This is confirmed by the following data showing that farms with little sown area were the ones hiring implements:

TABLE 28

PERCENTAGES OF FARMS RENTING STOCK

	Without sown area or with up to 2 *des.*	With sown area over 2 *des.*
1917	7	5
1922	33	9

Thus the basic forms of dependence of the weak on the prosperous farms are the hiring of horses and the renting of stock, although this dependence is covered by the use among the peasants themselves of the terms 'family', 'friendly' or 'neighbourly' help.

There is also clear evidence of changes in the hiring of wage-labour (in open form):

TABLE 29

NUMBER OF FARMS HIRING

	Time-rate workers	Day- and piece-rate workers	Total
1917	17	13	30
1920	7	18	25
1922	3	31	34

Parallel to the decline in time-rate workers is the increase in day- and piece-rate workers, yet official statistics only record time-rate workers. (*Presumably this is why it appeared to Shanin to be next to nil, although in percentage terms the figure for this* volost' *was still pretty low.*) The number of farms engaged in the so-called *promysly* has also grown. There were 126 farms in 1917, 114 in 1920 and 148 in 1922. (*The term* promysly *is usually translated as 'handicrafts and trades'.*) The figures show that the extreme sown area groups, above all, are engaged in *promysly*, indicating the growth in the sale by the poor of their labour power.[10]

TABLE 30

PERCENTAGE OF FARMS WITH 'DOMESTIC PROMYSLY' WITHIN EACH
SOWN AREA GROUP

Without sown area	Up to 1 *des.*	1–2 *des.*	2–6 *des.*	6–10 *des.*	10–13 *des.*
60	28	22	15	20	50

Kritsman also reproduced further evidence of differentiation. Of 25 farms renting out their land in 1922, 19 had no livestock. In contrast, 232 farms (29 per cent of all farms) since the Revolution have constructed new buildings or made capital repairs to the old, all the more striking in an area without wood, which implies that such repairs or constructions require the purchase of at least the materials. The prosperous farms sell proportionately more grain:

TABLE 31

PERCENTAGE OF FARMS SELLING GRAIN WITHIN EACH
SOWN AREA GROUP

Without sown area	Up to 4 *des.*	4–8 *des.*	8–10 *des.*	10–13 *des.*
13	18	26	33	50

The research report also claimed that the tax in kind particularly hit the weakest farms, unlike the *razverstka* (requisition) system of the old economic policy. During 'War Communism' the president of the *sel'sovet* was usually a poor or middle peasant, according to the report, whereas under the NEP it was usually a prosperous peasant.

To sum up the study of Nikol'skaya Volost', the years 1920–1923 showed an indubitable process of proletarianisation (an increase in the proportion of farms without stock or livestock) and an increase in work with alien livestock and agricultural implements (so that the means of production were in essence being used as capital). This was a process of class stratification of the peasantry, at the same time as the grouping by sown area showed a sharp decline in the extreme groups, that is, an equalisation.

(ii) a Znamenskaya Volost', Tambov Gubernia

This study, like the preceding one, was conducted by Yakovlev and published in 1924. It is free from the undersampling error of the previous study and is more systematic, if less detailed. The sown area grouping gives the following stratification:

TABLE 32

PERCENTAGE OF FARMS WITH A SOWN AREA

	Without sown area and up to 0.1 *des.*	0.1–2 *des.*	2–4 *des.*	4–6 *des.*	6–10 *des.*	10–16 *des.*	16–25 *des.*	Total
1920	2.1	17.1	31.0	29.1	20.1	0.6	0	100
1923	5.7	17.9	25.8	23.8	22.1	4.2	0.5	100

Even using the criterion of sown area, the stratification process was more intense than this table indicates. (*He supported this claim by showing the proportion of the total sown area held by each sown area grouping, as well as the population in each sown area grouping. This is not reproduced here, but the population was, as Kritsman argues, concentrated in the smallest sown area groupings, and the total sown area of the smaller farms fell, even though the number of such farms grew. In my view, this is hardly compatible with Chayanov's biological life-cycle explanation of rural differentiation, although there was a population increase among the highest sown area farms* (*over 10* desyatins).) The average sown area per farm changed as follows:

TABLE 33

AVERAGE SOWN AREA PER FARM (IN *DESYATINS*) WITHIN EACH SOWN AREA GROUP

	0.1–2 *des.*	2–4 *des.*	4–6 *des.*	6–10 *des.*	10–16 *des.*	16–25 *des.*
1920	1.21	2.91	4.60	7.13	11.25	—
1923	1.03	2.89	4.82	7.38	11.28	19.00

At the same time there was, especially among the bourgeois peasantry, a fall in the old 'large families' and the establishment of a family of bourgeois type, as the following table shows:

TABLE 34

AVERAGE FAMILY SIZE PER FARM, WITHIN EACH SOWN AREA GROUP

	Without sown area and up to 0.1 *des.*	0.1–2 *des.*	2–4 *des.*	4–6 *des.*	6–10 *des.*	10–16 *des.*	16–25 *des.*
1920	4.3	3.8	4.5	6.3	8.9	13.7	—
1923	4.2	4.1	4.5	5.6	7.0	7.7	11.7

This indicates a complete change in the character of the sown area groups, as can be seen from changes in the sown area per person within each sown area group:

TABLE 35

CHANGES IN SOWN AREA PER PERSON (IN *DESYATINS*), WITHIN EACH SOWN AREA GROUP

	0.1–2 *des.*	2–4 *des.*	4–6 *des.*	6–10 *des.*	10–16 *des.*	16–25 *des.*
1920	0.32	0.65	0.73	0.80	0.82	—
1923	0.25	0.64	0.86	1.05	1.46	1.62

This is a whole revolution. The difference between the average sown area per person in the lowest and highest groups changed from 2½ times in 1920 to 6½ times in 1923. The commodity character of the highest groups is indicated by the fact that in them are concentrated the special crops, as was evident in the case of flax:

TABLE 36

DISTRIBUTION OF FARMS, TOTAL SOWN AREA AND FLAX PRODUCTION

	Without sown area and up to 2 *des.*	2–6 *des.*	6–10 *des.*	Over 10 *des.*	Total
Farms	24	49	22	5	100
Total sown area	4	44	38	14	100
Flax production	0	32	43	25	100

The highest sown area groups also predominate in terms of productive livestock:

TABLE 37

PERCENTAGE OF FARMS, POPULATION, SOWN AREA AND LIVESTOCK, WITHIN EACH SOWN
AREA GROUP FOR 1920 AND 1923*

		Farms	Population	Sown area	Pigs	Young horned livestock	Grown sheep	Cows
Without sown area	1920	19.2	12.6	5.2	25.0	25.0	5.1	13.7
and up to 2 *des.*	1923	23.6	18.0	4.3	15.4	13.2	7.4	16.1
2–6 *des.*	1920	60.1	55.4	56.9	50.0	50.0	55.1	60.8
	1923	49.6	46.1	44.1	19.2	43.9	38.0	47.9
6–10 *des.*	1920	20.1	30.6	36.2	25.0	25.0	38.0	24.6
	1923	22.1	28.6	38.0	34.6	33.7	41.5	28.3
Over 10 *des.*	1920	0.6	1.4	1.7	0	0	1.4	0.9
	1923	4.7	7.3	13.6	30.8	9.2	13.1	7.7

*each column for each year totals 100 per cent.

However, it is worth attempting a comparison of farms without sown area and farms without livestock:

TABLE 38
PERCENTAGE OF FARMS

	Without sown area	Without working livestock	Excess of those without working livestock over those without sown area
1920	2.1	29.9	27.8
1923	5.7	51.2	45.5

This indicates that there was a colossal growth in the number of farms being run with alien working livestock. The loss of working livestock was borne primarily by the lowest sown area groups:

TABLE 39
PERCENTAGE OF FARMS WITHOUT WORKING LIVESTOCK, WITHIN EACH SOWN AREA GROUP

	Without sown area and up to 0.1 *des.*	0.1–2 *des.*	2–4 *des.*	4–6 *des.*	6–10 *des.*	Over 10 *des.*
1920	85.7	67.5	37.7	13.8	4.5	—
1923	97.4	91.1	69.7	34.1	15.1	—

The same process was indicated by the number of working horses per farm (not reproduced here), but the evidence of class differentiation in terms of stock was not so clear: in 1920 37.1 per cent of farms had no stock at all, as against 37.7 in 1923. Similarly for complex machinery, 86.8 per cent of the farms had none in 1920, as against 89.6 per cent in 1923. However, the stock tended over the three years to become concentrated in the highest sown area groups. Kritsman showed this in various tables, but I have chosen one which compared working horses with ploughs and complex machinery in percentage terms, which makes it comparable with Table 37:

TABLE 40

PERCENTAGE OF WORKING HORSES, PLOUGHS AND COMPLEX MACHINERY, WITHIN EACH
SOWN AREA GROUP FOR 1920 AND 1923*

		Working horses	Ploughs	Complex machinery
Without sown area	1920	7.1	3.1	4.2
and up to 2 *des.*	1923	3.3	1.5	0
2–6 *des.*	1920	57.6	47.3	38.9
	1923	44.5	31.6	13.2
6–10 *des.*	1920	33.3	47.3	52.1
	1923	39.0	47.8	53.8
Over 10 *des.*	1920	2.0	2.3	4.8
	1923	13.2	19.1	33.0

*each column for each year totals 100 per cent.

These figures seem to corroborate the analysis of the distribution of stock and livestock by Grosskopf based on figures referring to the overall economy.

One can summarise these results as follows: the lowest sown area groups (up to 2 *desyatins*) have lost a little sown area, but a great deal of stock and livestock, and are thus using alien means of production. The middle groups (2–6 *desyatins*) have lost sown area, but this has been offset by the decline in the number of farms and in population; however, the loss of stock has been much greater than the loss of sown area. In the group with 6–10 *desyatins,* the position is not definite. The highest groups (over 10 *desyatins*) has a concentration, not only of sown area (officially), but also stock and livestock.

TABLE 41

ESTIMATE OF THE SOWN AREA OF FARMS WITHOUT LIVESTOCK

	Sown area in *des.*	(a) as a percentage of total sown area	Excess of no. of farms without livestock over no. of farms without sown area	(c) as a percentage of total no. of farms
	(a)	(b)	(c)	(d)
1920	487	18½	186	28
1923	913	31	314	46
Percentage increase	+87		+69	

The data do not allow the grouping by livestock, nor the comparison of the extent of the farms (sown area) with the extent of means of production. But if one proceeds from the number of farms without working livestock and from the average sown area per farm within each sown area group, it is possible to estimate the sown area of farms without livestock; see Table 41. Thus the number of farms being run without working livestock has grown, but their sown area has grown more quickly and the capitalist farms in this way hold in their hands almost half the farms with almost one third of the sown area. Farms with insufficient livestock were not counted in this calculation, nor were farms with no stock or not enough stock, nor, finally, were the open forms of capitalist exploitation (day- and time-rate labour). On the basis of this picture of concentration of the means of production in the highest sown area groups, one can use the data available to describe the inter-relations between the groups.

Between 1920 and 1923, over eight per cent of the households emigrated or were liquidated; two-thirds of these farms in 1920 had no horses, and four-fifths of them had no stock. The same can be seen from the sown area groupings:

TABLE 42
PERCENTAGE OF HOUSEHOLDS WHICH EMIGRATED OR
BECAME EXTINCT, 1920–1923

Without sown area	Up to 2 des.	2–4 des.	4–6 des.	6–10 des.	10–16 des.
86	23	6	1.5	0.8*	0

*this is an estimate since the figure given is 'less than 1'

The farms without sown area in 1920 almost completely disappeared during the three years, and since the number of such farms almost trebled up to 1923 (*see Table 32*) this was because of other farms losing their sown area. Farms without means of production are compelled to rent it: 80 per cent of farms hiring horses are horseless farms, or to put it another way, 67 per cent of all horseless farms hire livestock of some kind (74 per cent if one excludes farms without sown area which were effectively not being run as farms). Of the remaining horseless farms (those not hiring stock) most plough by some other means: cow, bullock, pulling a scraper by hand, or harnessing themselves to the plough. Clearly these 'independent' farms are ones which could find no buyer for their labour power. The renting of stock shows a similar pattern: of those renting stock, 73 per cent are horseless farms, and 27 per cent are farms with horses. *After a critique of a table showing the hiring of stock, livestock and workers according to a conventional definition of poor, middle and prosperous peasants* (bednyaki, serednyaki, zazhitochnye), *a critique which showed that the peasant running his own farm was one step from giving it up and renting out the land, Kritsman examined the renting of land for arable or fodder purposes:*

TABLE 43
RENTING OF LAND BY SOWN AREA GROUPS

	Up to 2 des.	2–6 des.	6–10 des.	Over 10 des.	Total
Farms	24	49	22	5	100
Sown Area	4	44	38	14	100
Rented Arable Land	1	28	47	24	100
Rented Haymaking Land	0	19	48	33	100

Thus the farms with highest sown area are renting in extra land, particularly for haymaking. All farms over 10 *desyatins* are renting extra land, as are 77.6 per cent of farms between six and 10 *desyatins*. Even state land is being rented by the peasants, and between one-third and one half of the weakest farms are renting out land, that is, no less than 15 per cent of all farms.

There are no data on wage-labour, but data are available on the so-called *promysly*. The number of farms engaged in *promysly* declined slightly between 1920 and 1923; in percentage points the decline was from 22.2 per cent to 20.9 per cent. However, closer examination reveals a different aspect to this decline:

TABLE 44
FARMS WITH *PROMYSLY*

		Without sown area and up to 0.1 des.	0.1–2 des.	2–4 des.	4–6 des.	6–10 des.	10–16 des.	Total	Overall percentage
Number of	1920	7	43	46	33	19	0	148	22.2
farms	1923	37	53	25	14	14	1	144	20.9
Percentage	1920	50	38	22	17	14	—	—	22.2
of farms	1923	95	43	14	9	9	3	—	20.9
Percentage of men	1920	42	36	21	13	6	—	—	16.2
working in *promysly*	1923	83	45	14	6	6	2	—	16.4

Thus *promysly* are not 'trades' and 'crafts' in the sense applicable to an 'independent' farm. The highest sown area farms are most engaged in special crop production (*see Table 36*), yet their commitment to *promysly* declined, and the percentage of male workers engaged in *promysly* rose dramatically among the lowest sown area groups from 1920 to 1923. (*Kritsman does not say so, in so many words, but it is reasonable to conclude that this was a hidden form of wage-labour.*)

The prosperous farms also make most use of cooperation:

TABLE 45
FARM MEMBERSHIP OF COOPERATIVES IN 1923*

	Without sown area and up to 0.1 *des.*	0.1–2 *des.*	2–4 *des.*	4–6 *des.*	6–10 *des.*	10–16 *des.*	16–25 *des.*	Total	Overall percentage
Number of farms in cooperatives	7	16	29	74	116	29	4	275	—
Percentage of all farms in cooperatives	2.5	6	10.5	27	42	10.5	1.5	100	—
Percentage of all farms within sown area group	18	13	16	45	76	100	100	—	40
*Distribution of farms not in cooperatives	8	25.5	36	21.5	9	0	0	100	

The highest sown area groups (over 10 *desyatins*) are all members of cooperatives. Although only five per cent of all farms, they are 12 per cent of cooperative members. Comparing the middle row with the distribution of farms not in cooperatives, it is clear that more than half the cooperative members have a sown area of over six *desyatins,* whereas almost 70 per cent of the non-members have less than four *desyatins.* The research report claimed that these cooperatives were only used as a cover for the large-scale peasants to rent government land. The poor peasants' share in these cooperatives were *de facto* the property of their rich relatives, according to the research report. Deliveries at the local railway station for one cooperative, for example, were not transported to the village cooperatively. Each farm had to transport its own seed loan from the station for itself. No-one, not even a relative, carried the seed free to any horseless farm. The transport charges were quite high. Similarly in the autumn each farm had to carry away its own harvest independently. The attitude of the peasants not entering cooperatives (due to poverty) to the agricultural cooperatives was very hostile. Sometimes wage-labourers were described by those hiring them as members of the *artel'.* However, some of the *artely* were typically composed of *serednyaki.* The prosperous also used the Committees of Mutual Aid, and predominated among the leadership. These committees only helped themselves and were composed of those who needed no help. Only those who could provide shoes and clothes for their children sent them to school. Even the tax burden fell most heavily on the poor, since they paid tax on the harvest they paid to those who had ploughed their land, or on the harvest of the land they had rented out, whereas the larger farms renting the land, who disposed of the harvest, paid no tax on it.

In general, the analysis of Znamenskaya Volost' confirms the analysis of the data from the other regions. Thus the stratification of the peasantry took place significantly more quickly than could be judged from the movements in the percentages of the extreme sown area groupings. This circumstance is not surprising, for the grouping was produced on the basis of data of sown area of 'one's own' farm juridically, and not in the economic sense of sown area, and hence were consciously distorted by the population.

(ii) b Pavlodarskaya Volost', Tambov Gubernia

This analysis is based on a report by G. Dronin [*Krest'yanskoe*, 1923] which suffers from the same problem as the Nikol'skaya Volost'. It counted only farms existing in 1922 and did not count farms which had been liquidated by 1922. For 1917 this undersampling comprised 11.4 per cent of all farms, and 10.8 per cent of the population. The significance of this for the weak farms can be seen by comparing their distribution on various indices in the survey with their distribution in the agricultural census:

TABLE 46
PERCENTAGES OF FARMS IN 1917

	Without sown area	Without working livestock	Without cows
Survey	4.5	21.4	12.5
Census	13.5	33.5	24.3

The sown area grouping shows the following changes:

TABLE 47
PERCENTAGES OF FARMS WITH SOWN AREA

	Without sown area	Up to 1 des.	1–2 des.	2–4 des.	4–7 des.	7–10 des.	10–15 des.	Over 15 des.	Total
1917	4.5	7.0	18.0	32.9	22.5	9.4	3.5	2.2	100
1920	3.0	3.5	17.3	42.2	28.0	5.3	0.7	—	100
1922	3.4	6.2	18.4	36.1	27.4	6.6	1.8	1.0	100

Evidently there was an equalisation from 1917 to 1920 and stratification from 1920 to 1922, but the grouping by working livestock bears a different character:

TABLE 48
PERCENTAGE OF FARMS WITH WORKING LIVESTOCK

	Without working livestock	With 1 horse	With 2 horses	With 3 horses	With 4 horses and more	Total
1917	21.4	43.3	27.7	5.3	2.3	100
1920	36.3	49.4	13.0	1.2	0.3	100
1922	49.3	46.4	4.2	0.1	—	100

The *volost'* suffered quite a lot in 1920–1 from banditry which killed off a significant part of the working and other livestock.

TABLE 49
DISTRIBUTION OF STOCK AMONG FARMS: PERCENTAGES

	Without any agricultural stock	Without plough or *sokha**	With *sokha* & without plough	With plough & without *sokha*	With plough and *sokha*	Total
1917	23.8	3.5	29.9	6.9	35.9	100
1920	29.2	4.9	27.1	9.7	29.1	100
1922	33.0	8.1	23.1	10.1	25.7	100

*The *sokha* was a kind of wooden plough.

Judging by these groupings there was a general process of impoverishment. One can show the actual situation by comparing farms without sown area, farms without stock, and farms without livestock:

TABLE 50
PERCENTAGES OF FARMS

	Without sown area	Without working livestock	Excess of farms without livestock over farms without sown area	Without *sokha* or plough*	Excess of farms without *sokha* or plough over farms without sown area
1917	4.5	21.4	16.9	27.3	22.8
	(13.5)	(33.5)	(20.0)		
1920	3.0	36.3	33.3	34.1	31.1
1922	3.4	49.3	45.9	41.1	37.7

*This appears to be columns 1 and 2 of Table 49 added together.

There has thus been a clear and quite significant growth in farms without stock or livestock which are nevertheless running as farms. The figures in brackets are those of the agricultural census, so the effects of undersampling are not too great in this respect. There is a difference between the compulsory use of means of production by the poor in the early post-revolutionary years and the later, dependent use of stock and livestock. However, the compulsion was not heavy in the early years since many of the poor were at the front. There is only anecdotal evidence in the report on the hiring of livestock and stock, but apparently the conditions for doing so are burdensome. The peasantry are concentrating on repair and construction work of their own farms, despite the lack of wooden materials. The horseless farms cannot gather the wood, and are giving themselves into servitude in buying ready-made constructions. The report mentions the development of renting land of up to nine, 13 and even 18 *desyatins* and says: 'The conditions of exploitation of labour and of renting land out of the state funds and from the *sovkhozy* favour the process of growth

of a new bourgeoisie . . . at the expense of the Soviet state and the poor.' The
report claims that those hanging on to farms did so because there was not
enough work outside the farm, and that this process could not last for long.
While not objecting to this as the reason for the poor staying on their farms, one
must point out that the situation is that the poor are running their farms with
alien means of production, a hidden form of proletarianisation which accounts
for the relatively few farms without sown area, and which shows why this state
of affairs could be a long-lasting one.

The Pavlodarskaya Volost' research is interesting because it gives the
chance to compare the groupings by sown area, working livestock and stock
with the general grouping by wealth which it also uses. The wealth groups are
defined as follows (*with Kritsman's punctuation*):

'(1)   Prosperous—those with full (?) presence of livestock, both working and
       productive (!), and with a male work force and agricultural stock.
(2)   Middle—those with a partial (?) presence of the above.
(3)   Weak—those with a lack of working livestock, a small quantity of
       productive livestock and a decline (?) in agricultural stock. *Promysly,* as
       a rare phenomenon, is only taken into account in the *volost'* when the
       degree of prosperity depends on it.'

This definition of degree of wealth gives the following results:

TABLE 51
PERCENTAGE OF FARMS

	Prosperous	Middle	Weak	Total
1917	23.0	47.2	29.8	100
1922	4.5	38.2	57.3	100

The effects of this theoretical vagueness can be shown by comparing the
percentages of 'weak' farms with other relevant indices:

TABLE 52
COMPARISON OF PERCENTAGES OF FARMS

	Weak	Without working livestock	Without plough or *sokha*	Without sown area	Without sown area and up to 2 *des.*	Without sown area and up to 4 *des.*
1917	29.8	21.4	27.3	4.5	29.5	62.4
1922	57.3	49.3	41.1	3.4	28.0	64.1

Neither the farms without horses nor those without stock exhaust the
number of weak farms dependent on other farms, which apparently include
those farms with stock but without livestock, and vice versa. In 1917 the lack
of stock seemed fundamental, but in 1922 it was the lack of livestock which
placed the weak in great dependence on the more powerful households (the

impossibility not only of cultivating the land, but also of transporting both produce and things bought in). The comparison shows that neither in 1917 nor in 1922 did the number without sown area correspond to the weak, but if in 1917 those with no sown area or up to two *desyatins* roughly corresponded to the weak, then in 1922 it was those with up to four *desyatins.* In other words, those sowing two to four *desyatins* had changed from petit-bourgeois to proletarian farms (although hidden).

On the basis of a similar comparison for the prosperous, one can conclude that if in 1917 not all two-horse farms were prosperous, in 1922 all farms with two or more horses were prosperous. In 1917 most farms with a plough and *sokha* were prosperous, but in 1922 this was not enough to be prosperous. It is more difficult to draw conclusions about the middle peasants; in 1917 they roughly coincided with the numbers owning one horse, whereas in 1922 some of those with one horse (evidently those lacking stock) were weak. At the same time there was an increase in the proportion of middle farms with a plough and *sokha* by 1922, and their sown area also increased. This raises doubts about the definition of middle farms: the partial presence of necessary means of production could mean that they are insufficient in the means of production, that is, weak farms. In addition, a small quantity of productive livestock (yet with the necessary means of production) could mean that they are actually middle farms being independent but not exploiting. Yet despite all the inadequacies of the data on the Pavlodarskaya Volost', it shows the same process of stratification as the more detailed data collected earlier.

C. THE TRANSVOLGA: MALOTOLKAEVSKAYA VOLOST', SAMARA GUBERNIA

This is based on a report by M. Prokontsev [*Krest'yanskoe,* 1923]. The data on this *volost'* are very scanty. There was 22 per cent undersampling of farms in 1917, and 30 per cent in 1920. The *volost'* has undergone famine and from 1920 to 1922 lost almost half its working horses, two-fifths of its cows, almost three-quarters of its sheep, more than 90 per cent of its pigs, and one quarter of its ploughs and machines. The sown area grouping gives the following results:

TABLE 53
PERCENTAGE OF FARMS WITH A SOWN AREA

	Without sown area	Up to 1 *des.*	1–3 *des.*	3–5 *des.*	5–7 *des.*	7–10 *des.*	10–15 *des.*	Over 15 *des.*	Total
1917	1	6	26	25	19	12	6	5	100
1920	2	13	44	26	10	4	1	—	100
1922	4	19	50	19	6	2	0	—	100

This shows an apparent overall decline in sown area.

Other groupings were not produced by the survey, unfortunately, but there is a comparison of the number of farms, working horses and agricultural stock:

TABLE 54

NUMBER OF FARMS, WORKING HORSES AND AGRICULTURAL STOCK

	Farms	Working horses	Ploughs	Agricultural machinery
1917	889	2040	927	830
1920	997	1553	947	857
1922	1054	784	703	596

Clearly, a significant part of the peasantry in 1922 conducted their farms with the help of alien working horses and agricultural stock. In particular it can be noted that the report said that for ploughing, two or more horses were harnessed together (the ploughs were two-horsed, the soil was solid). In 1922, almost half the farms had no working livestock, as the following table shows:

TABLE 55

DISTRIBUTION OF FARMS, LIVESTOCK AND STOCK IN 1922

	Farms	Number of working horses	Ploughs	Machines
Prosperous	157	297	209	258
Middle	419	416	670	287
Weak	478	71	124	51
Total	1054	784	1003	596

(*This suggests that the 1922 figure for ploughs in Table 54 should be 1,003, but there are few misprints in this work.*) The table demonstrates that around 410 (weak) farms had no working livestock (that is, around 39 per cent of farms), and about 354 had no ploughs (of whom 41 had no sown area). *Kritsman paid no other attention to the grouping by wealth because it was not shown in the report how the categories were defined.* The report claims that the costs to the poor of hiring livestock were extraordinarily high, but that the prosperous paid a low rent to the poor who rented out land to them. It also claims that the poor, not having the strength to cope with the land which remained after the distribution according to the number (in the family), were compelled to give their allotment to peasants with horses and stock, either for rent or for cultivation. The poor often worked as day workers not because they needed to, but to 'work off' (as a way of paying for) the use of horses, stock, seed grain and other things. The prosperous parts of the peasantry often bought horses in Siberia. The following data on the interrelation of time-rate and day workers are interesting:

TABLE 56
THE HIRE OF WORKERS

	Time-rate in person-months	Day-rate in person-months
1917	635	519
1922	41	483

Time-rate working has almost been extinguished, but day working has hardly diminished, being used during harvesting and threshing. The count of hired labour, especially day workers, is without doubt not complete for 1922 (and was far from full for day workers in 1917) but it does express the change in the hiring of time-rate workers. If it is counted in person-months (at 25 working days in a month), then the open hiring of labour on a daily basis was three per cent in 1917 and 32 per cent in 1922.

D. THE UKRAINE: SHAMRAEVSKAYA VOLOST', KIEV GUBERNIA

This analysis is based on a report by Z. Tsybul'skii [*Krest'yanskoe,* 1923]. There was no undersampling, compared to the agricultural census. It was correctly remarked in the report that Kiev Gubernia was the region of the sugar industry, which has a great influence on the peasant economy. In the town of Shamraevka itself there is a sugar factory which is starting to have an economic relation with the peasantry. Nevertheless, there was not a sound in the report on the sown area of sugar beet or its distribution. There was the usual banal sown area grouping without understanding that the sown area of beetroot is the determining feature of a sugar beet region. The sown area grouping gives the following picture of equalisation, slowing down in the period 1920–2:

TABLE 57
PERCENTAGE OF FARMS WITH SOWN AREA

	Without sown area	Up to ½ des.	From ½–1 des.	1–2 des.	2–3 des.	3–5 des.	5–8 des.	Over 8 des.	Total
1917	10.8	5.9	14.8	39.4	15.4	11.0	2.2	0.5	100
1920	3.7	2.9	15.2	49.4	17.4	9.8	1.5	0.1	100
1922	3.8	2.9	17.7	48.0	17.0	9.2	1.3	0.1	100

The grouping by working livestock bears a similar character:

TABLE 58
PERCENTAGE OF FARMS WITH WORKING LIVESTOCK

	Without working livestock	With 1 head	With 2 head	With 3 head	With 4 head	Total
1917	46	8	43	1.0	2.0	100
1920	45	14	38	1.5	1.5	100
1922	49	28	22	0	0	99

TABLE 59
PERCENTAGE OF FARMS WITH STOCK

	Without any stock	Without plough	With plough	Total
1917	50.0	20.3	29.7	100
1920	54.2	20.8	25.0	100
1922	55.4	21.6	23.0	100

Thus in 1922 all ploughs were concentrated in the hands of less than one quarter of the farms. The comparison of farms without sown area, without livestock and without ploughs gives the following results:

TABLE 60
PERCENTAGE OF FARMS

	Without sown area	Without working livestock	Excess of farms without working livestock over farms without sown area	Without ploughs	Excess of farms without ploughs over farms without sown area
1917	10.8	46	35.2	70.3	59.5
1920	3.7	45	41.3	75.0	71.3
1922	3.8	49	45.2	77.0	73.2

Apparently almost half the farms are running without working livestock, but the report provides no data on this. The following comparison indicates the hiring of stock:

TABLE 61
PERCENTAGE OF FARMS

	Without ploughs	Excess of farms without ploughs over farms without sown area	Renting in agricultural stock	Without working livestock
1917	70.3	59.5	51.3	46
1920	75.0	71.3	63.8	45
1922	77.0	73.2	76.4	49

The percentage of farms renting in stock is colossal and rises in proportion with the excess of farms without ploughs over the percentage without sown area, showing that it is an economic necessity. Even some of the farms with working livestock rent in stock – in fact, more than half of them in 1922. The report says that the one-horse peasant is a *serednyak* (middle peasant) of a new type who is trying to move into the 'present-day *serednyaki*', and supports the latter (the two-horse peasant). He lives in friendship with the 'present-day *serednyak*' for he uses (for a 'working off' payment, of course) a plough, a cultivator and a chaff-cutter. One must point out that since no farms had more than two horses in 1922, the 'present-day *serednyak*' with two horses disposes of almost two-thirds of the horses, although they are only one quarter of the farms. One has to look among them for those who are exploiting, to some degree or other, three quarters of the peasantry. The political effects of this are, according to the report, that the one-horse peasant feels himself strong, fearing neither the horseless peasant nor the local powers, and together with the two-horse peasants runs the village.

There is also a grouping by wealth in the report (weak, prosperous, middle) which shows how careful one must be with such a grouping. Among the 'weak' are 133 farms with two horses, almost half the two-horse farms. The report then excludes them on the grounds that they were middle peasants! The report says that the peasants themselves considered the two-horse peasants as middle peasants.

E. THE INDUSTRIAL CENTRE AND NORTH WEST

(i) Yaropol'skaya Volost', Moscow Gubernia
The data on both these industrial regions are quite unsatisfactory and take no account of the influence on the class stratification of the peasantry of the basic features of these regions: industrial crops, livestock rearing and the non-agricultural occupations of the peasantry. The most detailed data are those on Yaropol'skaya Volost', largely thanks to the fact that two investigations were conducted. The first, in 1922, was by P. Gurov [*Krest'yanskoe,* 1923] and the second, in 1924, was by F. Kretov [1925]. It is only possible to compare them in rare cases, since the first contains data on 1917, 1920 and 1922, while the second predominantly concerns 1915, 1923 and 1924 (and only sometimes 1912, 1920 and 1922). Besides, each author tends to remain silent on the issues discussed by the other. The earlier 1922 investigation only counts farms existing in 1922, excluding farms liquidated between 1917 and 1922, but undersampling is only 6 per cent for 1917, 1920 and 1922.[11] For this reason the comparison of the number of farms and sown area in 1917, and the number of farms and working livestock for 1920 does not show a special under-sampling of the weak farms:

TABLE 62

| | 1917 | | 1920 | |
	Farms	Sown area	Farms	Working livestock
Counted	94.0	93.7	94.6	96.0
Not counted	6.0	6.3	5.4	4.0

A direct comparison for the 1922 research shows a certain undersampling of farms without working livestock, and without cows, and a more significant undersampling of farms without sown area:

TABLE 63
PERCENTAGE OF FARMS

	Without working livestock		Without sown area	Without cows	
	1917	1920	1917	1917	1920
Agricultural Census	16.0	15.1	7.2	12.5	11.3
1922 Research	12.7	12.8	3.7	9.4	9.3

The apparent undersampling of farms without cows is possibly because 100 farms have somehow disappeared from the distribution of farms by number of cows, and it is not clear from which grouping they have been lost. Both investigations for Yaropol'skaya Volost' give almost no data on the industrial crops or on the non-agricultural occupations of the peasantry. In the 1922 research there was only the remark, unsupported by data, that for the five-year period from 1917 to 1922 the number of farms with *promysly* and the number of people occupied in seasonal and local *promysly* had grown.

In the 1924 study, one finds (besides the remark that 'the peasantry receives its means of subsistence from agriculture, from earnings on the side and to an insignificant degree from handicraft *promysly'*) the following data on the number of passports issued to people going out to get earnings:

TABLE 64
1924 STUDY: NUMBER OF PASSPORTS ISSUED

	Number of passports	As a percentage of the number of farms
1913	2357	—
1914	2730	(136 per cent of the number of farms in 1915)
1921	269	—
1922	115	5.4
1923	480	21.7
1924	893	38.2

Clearly there was a rapid revival in the proportion going out to work after 1922, but there is no grouping of farms on this basis. The figures refer to both men and women. This is clearly a region of people primarily occupied outside their farms as workers. There was a growth in the sown area and in the amount of productive livestock, but not horses, after the Revolution: this process started in 1921 or 1922. Taking 1915 as 100 for sown area, and 1914 as 100 for livestock:

TABLE 65
CHANGES IN CROPS AND LIVESTOCK

	Sown area				Livestock			
	Rye	Oats	Potatoes	All sown area	Cows	Sheep	Pigs	Horses
1923	105	47	104	93	135	208	63	100
1924	120	152	165	128	143	275	310	99

This growth was composed of the growth in the farms of actual farm owners (middle and prosperous) and of the increase in sown area and productive livestock of the essentially unemployed (including many demobilised Red Army men), running their farm of necessity and going off to the city as soon as the possibility opened up. In fact the growth in sown area and its transition to the pre-war level arrived in 1925 when the practice of leaving (for the town) was already quite widespread.

On flax cultivation the 1922 study only gives remarks in brackets such as 'Flax cultivation is highly developed in this region' or 'Here flax is a quite important factor in peasant commodity circulation'. There was a rapid growth in the number of farms selling flax:

TABLE 66
1922 STUDY: PERCENTAGE OF FARMS

	Selling flax	n	Selling, but not buying, grain	n
1917	7.6	—	2.3	—
1920	17.2	332	7.9	152
1922	31.4	640	5.6	113

Thus with a reduction in the percentage of farms selling grain, there was a sharp increase in the percentage of farms selling flax. In the 1924 research, there is the following data on sown area of flax (in *desyatins*):

TABLE 67
1924 STUDY: SOWN AREA OF FLAX

1915	1921	1922	1923	1924
1557	578	663	700	928

Thus there was a direct growth from 1921 to 1924 of 61 per cent. However, there is no grouping by flax cultivation in this study either.

There was also a significant growth in pig and sheep rearing, according to the 1924 study (*which differs somewhat on pigs from the 1922 study in brackets*):

TABLE 68
1924 STUDY: LIVESTOCK REARING

	Pigs	Sheep
1914	807	1672
1915	360	1097
(1917)	(451)	—
(1920)	(496)	—
1922	153	2565
(1922)	(705)	—
1923	509	3474
1924	2505	4591

Again there is no grouping in terms of these indices. In the 1922 study there was a grouping by sown area (*Kritsman pointed out various minor problems with this table*):

TABLE 69
1922 STUDY: PERCENTAGE OF FARMS WITH SOWN AREA

	Without sown area	Up to 1 des.	1–2 des.	2–3 des.	3–4 des.	4–5 des.	5–7 des.	7–10 des.	10–15 des.	Total
1917	3.7	7.1	20.8	29.5	18.0	9.9	8.0	2.0	0.9	100
1920	3.4	7.7	21.3	28.6	19.2	9.7	7.9	2.1	0.1	100
1922	3.4	7.6	24.4	28.1	17.7	9.7	6.9	2.1	0.1	100

There is no grouping by sown area in the 1924 study, but grouping by working livestock gives the following results:

TABLE 70
1924 STUDY: PERCENTAGE OF FARMS WITH WORKING LIVESTOCK

	Without working livestock	With 1 horse	With 2 horses	With 3 horses	With 4 or more	Total
1915	29.5	47.8	20.2	2.1	0.4	100
1920	15.1	72.5	12.1	0.3	—	100
1923	11.8	77.9	9.9	0.3	—	100
1924	13.4	76.3	10.0	0.3	—	100

There is no grouping by stock in either study, but in the 1922 study the percentage of farms without ploughing equipment is given:

TABLE 71
1922 STUDY: PERCENTAGE OF FARMS
WITHOUT PLOUGHING EQUIPMENT

1917	1920	1922
11.3	11.8	12.6

Kritsman combined the tables on the grouping by number of cows, although he was aware of various problems with this procedure: for example the 1922 study tended to undersample farms with two or more cows:

TABLE 72
BOTH STUDIES: PERCENTAGE OF FARMS WITH COWS

	Without cows	With 1 cow	With 2 cows	With 3 cows	With 4 and more cows	Total
1915	26.9	41.3	26.7	3.6	1.5	100
1920	11.3	55.4	32.0	1.2	0.1	100
1922	7.7	63.3	27.5	1.3	0.1	100
1923	5.9	60.2	30.7	3.0	0.2	100
1924	2.3	57.9	36.2	3.3	0.4	100

The figures are interpreted in the 1924 study as a 'general improvement in the material well-being of the peasantry', which implies a growth in the farms of all strata of the peasantry, but the decline in the number of farms without cows is paralleled by a growth in the number of horseless farms and in the number of passports issued to those leaving for paid employment. In a certain proportion of cases, what is happening is the growth of the domestic farm of workers and employees, usually in the care of their wives, so that the peasant can achieve a rise in living standards and improve the domestic farm by acquisition of a cow. Yet the farm, as the enterprise of an independent owner, has collapsed: from being petit-bourgeois, although very poor, he has been transformed into a proletarian, although his living standard has improved because of this. To a special degree this refers to peasants without horses, that is, without basic means of production.

I have noted earlier that the class stratification of the peasantry can appear in the form of the transition of farms with no sown area into sowing farms. Is class stratification now appearing in the form of the transition of farms without cows into farms with cows? It is necessary to avoid putting in the same pile those who live by the alienation of their labour power outside their own farm, and those who conduct their own farm (enterprise); that is, to distinguish the economic types of the proletarian and the petit-bourgeois. This is the first demand which must be put to the researcher, which he is obliged to fulfil, if he is not to 'play games with numbers'. Up to this time, unfortunately, this demand has always been transgressed. (*In a footnote, Kritsman cited evidence that children of the poor did not go to school since they had no clothes, no footwear and no text books.*)

The growth in proletarianisation is shown by the growth cited above in the farms without plough instruments and without horses. It can be seen from the comparison of the farms without sown area, without livestock and without stock:

TABLE 73

1922 STUDY: PERCENTAGES OF FARMS WITHOUT SOWN AREA, WORKING LIVESTOCK AND STOCK

	Without sown area	Without working livestock	Excess of farms without working livestock over farms without sown area	Without stock	Excess of farms without stock over farms without sown area
1917	3.7	12.8	9.1	11.3	7.6
1920	3.4	12.8	9.4	11.8	8.4
1922	3.4	11.9	8.5	12.6	9.2

Not surprisingly, the 1922 report states that the general number of farms renting in stock is growing continuously. The general number of implements and machines has grown.

According to the report, after the Revolution, and especially after the NEP, the prosperous and middle peasants by some means took over the machines, and the poor fell into the role of renting these machines, to be paid by 'working off' in the field, house or farmyard, although originally they had access to these machines on a friendly basis. The prosperous rented out at hiring points a large part of the complex machinery, but the middle and poor rented simple machines from their prosperous fellow-countrymen. The 1924 report only said one word on this issue: in the single official machine cooperative there were nine members and 40 ploughs and several other items of stock; that is, 4.4 ploughs per member!

The author of the 1924 study almost completely lacks a class approach to the analysis of the countryside, as can be seen from the fact that after introducing a table on the hiring of wage-labour by traders and the owners of dairy factories and other enterprises, he claimed that it shows that the base of the *kulak* was not in agriculture. This implies that a *kulak* is defined by the hiring of wage-labour.

TABLE 74

HIRING OF WAGE-LABOUR

	Yaropol'skaya Volost' (1924 Study)	Moscow Gubernia (Ts.S.U. data)
1923	0.7	1.1
1924	0.6	7.2

Clearly the *volost'* is not typical of the whole Moscow Gubernia, if the 1924 study is accurate. (*However, Kritsman demonstrated that wage-labour was also shown in data about workers and employees in rural cooperatives.*)

Apart from the significance of cows in some domestic farms, the growth (already indicated in Table 72) of the percentage of farms with more than three cows is somewhat more significant than it seems, since the average number of cows in farms with three or more grew from 3.7 in 1922 to 7.4 in 1923, and 7.9 in 1924. But dairy farming is only one direction in which Yaropol'skaya

Volost' is developing its commodity agriculture, it seems. Although there are no data on other branches of agriculture, there are data on the number of permits for construction:

TABLE 75
PERMITS FOR CONSTRUCTION

	Living accommodation	Outhouses
1915	13	5
1920	13	—
1921	22	1
1922	47	—
1923	84	70
1924	42	148

Thus the construction of houses suddenly declined after 1923 and the construction of economic (outhouse) buildings suddenly increased greatly in 1923. (*Kritsman refused to use the 1922 study's grouping by wealth, because there was no indication of how it was constructed or how it could be corrected – some of the mistakes may have been simply printing errors in the research report.*) Although these two reports do not give many of the most important data, nevertheless they can be used to show the growth of the class stratification of the peasantry.

(ii) Tsurikovskaya Volost', Smolensk Gubernia
This is based on a study by A. Vinogradov [*Krest'yanskoe*, 1923]. It only included 41 per cent of the farms in its sample, and also omitted those farms liquidated between 1917 and 1922. There is no agricultural census data available, so the extent of undersampling of particular groups cannot be estimated. From the research it is evident that in the *volost'* whole villages went off on paid carpentry work on occasions, but there are no numerical data on this. There are data for 1917, 1920 and 1922 only on agricultural stock:

TABLE 76
PERCENTAGE OF FARMS WITHOUT PLOUGHING
EQUIPMENT

1917	1920	1922
17	14	16

The report obscurely refers to 'horseless and stock-less (farms), who for the use of horses and stock give away part of the grain harvested by them'. It naïvely remarks that the farms without horses and without stock receive help from their closest relatives, so that the possibility of exploitation is reduced. But the 14 per cent in 1920 (and 16 per cent in 1922) of farms without stock signified a large growth in the number of exploited farms, because in 1920 they had compulsory access to the stock of the prosperous, but in 1922 this had already become impossible. Evidently, one-third of farms were engaged in *promysly;* that is, for every 100 farms there were 32 people so engaged in 1917, 1920 and 1922.

The best indication of the situation on working livestock is that the percentage of farms without it was 16.5 in 1917 and 11 per cent in 1922. According to a dynamic study, the percentage of farms without working livestock for the whole Smolensk gubernia was 10.9 in 1920 and 12.4 in 1922. Evidently the percentage of farms without livestock changed from 1917 to 1922 in a manner analogous to the changes in farms without stock (*Table 76*), that is a reduction to 1920 and an increase to 1922.

How far the situation changed from 1920 to 1922 can be judged from the following statements of the report:

> The struggle for equalisation in the years 1918, 1919 and 1920 included villages occupied in going off for carpentry work. Here the victory of the weak was most complete. . . . In another region . . . impelled by tax pressure the weak in the year just past of 1922 went over on to a definite offensive with the aim of achieving equalisation. But there was already not enough time. Here and there the struggle was not completed. And where it was completed, it finished not with the victory of the poor, but a compromise with the prosperous.
>
> The taxes were heavy for the weak, not even mentioning those without livestock or without stock. Tax pressure above all hindered the weak farm from sustaining itself, and on the other hand, the relative weakness of taxes for the prosperous assisted them.

The research report has a grouping by wealth but it is not known how it was arrived at and it does not include all the farms studied without indicating which farms were excluded or why. According to this classification, the middle peasantry have the best chance of changing their farm into a *khutor,* which again shows the dangers of the banal approach to the peasantry.

(iii) Goritskaya Volost', Tver Gubernia

The data are somewhat better in the study conducted by A. Bol'shakov [1925] which includes liquidated farms. The main problem with the study is the introduction of the 1924 figures, which are not comparable due to a large increase in population and number of farms when the *volost'* was enlarged. (*Kritsman left the 1924 figures out of the tables.*) According to the report, formerly many went off on seasonal *promysly* to factories and plants, but at the time of the study factory and plant workers stayed at home willy-nilly. In 1913 the *volost'* had received 159,298 roubles in this way, but in 1924 only 14,638 roubles. Before the war there had been a large amount of bazaar trade, which was evidently in flax: in Goritskaya Volost' there had been a fair eight times a year with an annual turnover of a million roubles. In the *volost'* the percentage of sown area devoted to flax was as follows:

TABLE 77
PERCENTAGE OF SOWN AREA DEVOTED TO FLAX

1913	1920	1923
21	8	9

Unfortunately there is no grouping of the peasantry taking account of these features, but there is a classification by working livestock:

TABLE 78
PERCENTAGE OF FARMS WITH HORSES

	Without horses	With 1 horse	With 2 horses	With 3 horses	With 4 or more horses	Total
1916	31.5	54.6	12.8	0.7	0.4	100
1920	34.0	65.0	1.0	0.1	0	100.1
1922	33.2	66.1	0.7	0	0	100
1923	32.7	66.5	0.8	0	0	100

There is no grouping by sown area, only the percentage of farms with no sown area:

TABLE 79
PERCENTAGE OF FARMS

	Without sown area	Without horses	Excess of farms without horses over farms without sown area
1916	11.9	31.5	19.6
1920	13.2	34.0	20.8
1922	12.8	33.2	20.4
1923	11.9	32.7	20.8

In the bazaar trade of Goritsa, a large part is taken up by cow butter (1,000 puds against 3,500 puds of rye). The following percentages were under grass:

TABLE 80
PERCENTAGE UNDER GRASS

1916	1920	1922	1923
3.9	0.2	1.3	1.5

For this reason, the classification by cattle is interesting:

TABLE 81
PERCENTAGE OF FARMS WITH CATTLE

	Without cattle	With 1 head	With 2 head	With 3 head	With 4 head	Total
1916	18.7	49.4	28.3	3.2	0.4	100
1920	18.3	48.8	28.8	3.7	0.4	100
1922	17.8	46.3	30.2	4.9	0.8	100
1923	16.6	45.8	31.4	4.5	0.7	100

Thus the increase in the proportion of farms with two or more cows is an indication of the developing commodity relations. This can be seen more clearly by showing the proportion of cattle owned by these groupings:

TABLE 82
DISTRIBUTION OF CATTLE AMONG DIFFERENT CATTLE-OWNING GROUPS

	Farms without cows & with 1 cow	Percentage of all cows owned by this group	Farms with 2 cows	Percentage of all cows owned by this group	Farms with 3 cows or more	Percentage of all cows owned by this group
1916	68.1	42.2	28.3	48.2	3.6	9.6
1920	67.1	41.3	28.8	48.0	4.1	10.7
1922	64.1	37.2	30.2	48.4	5.7	14.4
1923	62.4	35.5	31.4	48.9	6.2	15.7

The report also makes the interesting remark that the tax policy and line of conduct of the most important commissariat for the peasantry, The People's Commissariat of Agriculture, during the NEP has weakly supported the poorest farms, and weakly defended them from the stronger prosperous farms. The prosperous farms make better use of the cooperatives:

TABLE 83
PERCENTAGE OF FARMS IN COOPERATIVES IN 1924

	Without horses	With 1 horse	With 2 horses	With 3 or more	Not counted	Total
Among peasantry in cooperatives	9.0	84.0	2.5	0.3	4.2	100
Among the whole peasantry	27.0	71.4	1.6	0	—	100

Unfortunately, for the reasons indicated above, these data are insufficient to form a judgement on the class stratification in the *volost'*.

(iv) Prokzhinskaya Volost', Pskov Gubernia
The basis of this section is the study by A. Grafov [*Krest'yanskoe*, 1923]. The data are even more scanty than for the previous *volost'*. Only farms existing in

1922 were counted. It is impossible to estimate the undersampling of liquidated farms since there are no data from the agricultural census.

According to the report, 'the Pskov peasantry were an unfailing supply of labour power to the Petrograd factories and plants, and the remaining part of the free hands were used in farms cultivating flax', but neither of these circumstances are taken into account in the research. According to the report, the Pskov peasantry are now being suffocated by a surplus of labour power. It is interesting that, judging by the farms left in 1922, the main mass of land redistributions (54 per cent) and of returns (to the country) from the city (80 per cent) were in 1918. The following are the percentages of total sown area devoted to flax:

TABLE 84
PERCENTAGE OF TOTAL SOWN AREA
DEVOTED TO FLAX

1917	1920	1922
13	4.2	3.4

In 1923, it was expected to grow by one or two per cent, as against 1922. However, data on the number of farms selling flax show its growing significance since 1920:

TABLE 85
PERCENTAGE OF FARMS SELLING BUT
NOT BUYING

	Flax	n	Grain	n
1917	20	—	7	—
1920	2.5	31	2	26
1922	8.5	111	0.5	5

Consequently, despite what the report says, not all peasants are cautious in their approach to growing flax. There are also data on the growth of the renting of land:

TABLE 86
PERCENTAGE OF FARMS

	Renting in	Renting out
1917	37.7	15.8
1920	1.2	2.3
1922	3.8	1.4

According to the report, the forms of payment are varied: *metayage,* money, grain, hay, a field for tilling another field. There are cases when the poor receive livestock and stock and seed from the prosperous, but a large part of these deals are connected with the renting of land. Elsewhere the report remarks that there is a mass migration of peasants. Unfortunately there is no grouping by sown area of flax or by working livestock, nor even by sown area. There is only a grouping by wealth, and it is not known how it was arrived at. The prosperous are said in the report to be almost entirely traders, and are more friendly to Soviet power than before the NEP. The tax in kind, the new economic law, the opening of free trade and a series of other measures enable them to pursue their well-being unhindered.

Despite the inadequacies of the data on the *volosti* of the industrial regions, the root of which lies in the banal approach to the question, the data for some *volosti* confirm the growth of hidden capitalist exploitation, and in the others leave the question open for further investigation. Evidently, the grouping by stock has a basic significance for these regions (besides the special groupings, such as by flax or by cows). For two of the four *volosti* examined above on which there are data on the percentage of farms without stock (Tsurikovskaya and Yaropol'skaya) there was growth in the percentage from 1920 to 1922 of the farms without stock at the same time as the percentage of farms without livestock (for example, in Yaropol'skaya) fell somewhat. The percentage without stock in both *volosti* up to 1922 exceeded the percentage without livestock. The same phenomenon can be seen in the Shamraevskaya Volost' in Kiev Gubernia, where the sown area of sugar beet plays a big role. Only the analysis of the special groupings (by sown area of industrial crops, by cows and so on) can uncover the significance of this fact; in addition the analysis of the essentially separate matter of the domestic agriculture of industrial and other workers or small owners whose basic occupation is not cultivation would help clarify the significance of this fact, as would the separate analysis of the actual rural owner-cultivators; unfortunately there are no data on these matters in the studies of the above four *volosti*.

F. THE URALS: PETROVSKAYA VOLOST' IN THE BASHKIR REPUBLIC

The data on the Bashkir Republic are based on the unpublished report by S. Said-Galiev and refer to 1925, in comparison with 1912:

TABLE 87
PERCENTAGE OF FARMS

	Without sown area	Without horses	Excess of farms without horses over farms without sown area	Without cows
1912	27.7	18.7	− 9.0	24.0
1925	7.2	48.2	+41.0	30.5

This table describes in unusually clear fashion the sharp decline in farms without sown area and the huge increase in farms without horses. The enlarged

Petrovskaya Volost' is composed of three former economically different *volosti* – two cultivating and one livestock rearing. Hence the data on the three former *volosti* must be examined separately, using the same indices as the previous table for the two cultivating *volosti:*

TABLE 88

FORMER PETROVSKAYA VOLOST'

1912	7.0	12.2	+ 5.2	15.8
1925	0	43.7	+43.7	28.2

FORMER MAKAROVSKAYA VOLOST'

1912	21.8	25.4	+ 3.6	31.5
1925	2.5	64.6	+62.1	41.2

FORMER GIREI-KONCHAKSKAYA VOLOST'

	Without sown area	Without horses	Without cows
1912	99.8	19.1	26.5
1925	98.0	65.3	38.0

The former Girei-Konchakskaya Volost' is purely livestock rearing and engaging in handicraft *promysly.* Because of the famine the population declined catastrophically by 61.5 per cent, working livestock by 94 per cent, large horned livestock by 76 per cent and other livestock by 93–5 per cent. The character of the change indicated above is quite distinct. For example, in the former Petrovskaya Volost' all provided themselves with sown area, but the proportion of horseless farms quadrupled, going to almost half of all farms. In the former Makarovskaya Volost' the percentage of farms with no sown area declined by almost nine times, while the percentage with no horses increased by 2.5 times, going up to almost two-thirds of the farms.

Kritsman also had recourse to a study of some villages in the Chelyabinksk and Perm areas, although he regarded it as 'not serious' and 'insignificant' [Lezhnev-Finkovskii and Savchenko, *1925*]. *It showed a lack of understanding of the stratification of the peasantry, since it constantly discussed distributions in terms of per farm averages of the whole sample.*

There is nothing on changes in the stratification of the peasantry. But there is a certain interest in the data on rural wage-labourers working on farms in the Etul'sku region: in 1915 they counted up 1,500 people, whereas in 1924 there were 900 to 1,000 people. Since there were 4613 households in the region, then there was at least one wage-labourer to every four or five households. The distribution of *batraki* (rural wage-labourers) by place of work was as follows:

TABLE 89

Worked	People	Percentage
In farms of Red Army men	52	7.5
In farms without labour power	48	7
In 15 dairy *artely*	62	9
For the more prosperous and *kulaks*	515	76.5
	677	100

That means that only in less than 15 per cent of cases can the hiring be explained by the lack of labour power in the family. The researchers argue for a reduction in the land available to peasants so that it would correspond to the fertiliser available and the smaller farms could be properly run! They also analyse the *khutory* quite separately from the village where they hired their wage-labour, with the result that class differentiation was less apparent. These four *khutory* in 1924 sowed 440 *desyatins*. There is also a quite strange commune which hires a significant amount of wage-labour. The better-off peasants receive on credit various machines which are very expensive. The most 'needy' receive ploughs, horses and grain on credit. Thus in the Perm area a process of stratification is taking place.

In the village of Starkii the distribution of farms in terms of arable land changed as follows:

TABLE 90
ARABLE LAND PER FARM

	From 1.5–2 *des.*	2–3 *des.*	3–4 *des.*	4–5 *des.*	5–6 *des.*	Over 6 *des.*	Total
Number of farms							
1923	—	5	14	9	3	1	32
1924	2	11	12	3	1	4	33

This indicates some differentiation, but there is no grouping by sown area. The amount of haymaking land increased by 46 per cent. This shift into haymaking was to avoid the tax on sown area, not arable land, indicating how statistics can express legal rather than economic changes. In 1923 there were three farms without horses, 28 with one horse and one with two horses, whereas in 1924 there were no farms without horses, 30 with one horse and three with two horses. In another village, Novye Tumachi, there were 10 horseless farms in 1923 and 1924, 16 farms with one horse in 1923 (18 in 1924) and one farm with two horses in 1924 only. The horseless farms paid for the hire of horses in grain, or by 'working off'. The data on sown area and arable land are in a complete mess, so no more can be gained from this study.

G. SIBERIA AND KAZAKHSTAN

(i) Shchuch'inskaya Volost', Akmolinskaya Gubernia

The data are taken from a document by A. Morosanov (of the Central Committee of the Russian Communist Party). The document was published in a shorter form in *Na Agrarnom Fronte* [*Morosanov,* 1925]. It contained data up to 1925. The *volost'* is characterised by an abundance of unsown land because of the colossal decline of sowing up to 1923. For this reason, the extent of individual peasant farms is here determined not by their land, but by their means of production. Taking 1917 data as 100, there is the following distribution (based on tax returns):

TABLE 91

	Number of farms	People	Sown area	Horses	Large horned livestock	Bullocks
1917	100	100	100	100	100	100
1920	113	105	91	126	128	118
1923	106	94	42	52	97	58
1924	112	96	47	54	101	49

In 1925 this process of restoration continued, as the following data on Shchuch'aya Station (1 April 1925) show as a percentage of 1923:

TABLE 92

	Farms	Horses	Large horned livestock	Bullocks
1923	100	100	100	100
1924	112	101	96	82
1925	110.5	111	96	108

The groupings by sown area and working livestock are only available for Shchuch'inskaya Volost' for 1923–4, so material for a judgement on the dynamics of stratification is only available for an interval of one year. To understand the actual character of the changes occurring, one must start with the centre of the *volost'*, Shchuch'aya Station, for which there are data for 1924–5 as well.

TABLE 93

PERCENTAGE OF HOUSEHOLDS, SHCHUCH'AYA STATION

	Without working livestock	With 1 head	With 2 head	With 3 head	With 4 head	With 5 head	With 6 head	Over 6 head	Total
1923	21.9	23.9	16.7	16.3	7.4	8.4	2.1	3.3	100
1924	29.6	26.7	15.8	14.4	5.6	4.8	1.4	1.7	100
1925	25.9	24.8	14.3	15.9	5.8	6.9	2.6	3.8	100

Thus there was a so-called movement downwards from 1923 to 1924 in the possession of livestock, and a so-called movement upwards from 1924 to 1925, but the result – although not so clear as the two movements – from 1923 to 1925 was differentiation. This conclusion is confirmed by data on the percentage of livestock within each livestock group:

TABLE 94
DISTRIBUTION OF LIVESTOCK WITHIN EACH LIVESTOCK GROUP

	Without working livestock	With 1 head	With 2 head	With 3 head	With 4 head	With 5 head	With 6 head	Over 6 head	Total
1923	—	11.3	15.7	22.8	13.7	19.3	5.9	11.3	100
1924	—	15.2	18.3	24.8	12.4	13.9	4.7	10.2	99.5
1925	—	11.9	13.7	23.0	10.9	16.7	7.3	16.5	100

The working livestock is concentrated in the highest groups. Because the differentiation is somewhat hidden by the movement downwards, it is especially unsatisfactory to limit oneself only to the percentage distribution of farms: more detailed data are necessary. The grouping by sown area for the whole *volost'* is as follows:

TABLE 95
CLASSIFICATION BY SOWN AREA

	Percentage of farms 1923	Percentage of farms 1924	Percentage of sown area 1923	Percentage of sown area 1924	Working livestock per farm in 1922
Without sown area	5.5	6.0	—	—	0.5
Up to 1 *des.*	28.4	25.6	9.1	7.1	0.46
1–2 *des.*	25.0	24.9	17.5	16.2	0.95
2–4 *des.*	25.34	26.7	32.0	32.7	1.95
4–6 *des.*	9.3	10.1	19.0	19.6	3.3
6–8 *des.*	3.8	4.1	10.8	11.6	4.2
8–10 *des.*	1.5	1.3	5.7	4.4	4.8
10–12 *des.*	0.6	0.5	2.7	2.3	5.2
12–15 *des.*	0.5	0.4	2.7	2.3	6.9
15–20 *des.*	0.03	0.2	0.2	2.2	8.9
Over 20 *des.*	0.03	0.2	0.3	1.6	6.4
Total	100	100	100	100	100

The researcher's conclusion that stratification has decreased is a hasty one. *Kritsman showed that there were problems in the report's treatment of the highest sown area groups, and consequently treated those with over 15* desyatins *as a single group for some purposes. Kritsman regrouped the table into the following groups: without sown area, up to two* desyatins, *2–8* desyatins, *8–15 desyatins, and over 15 desyatins. This gave an increase in the extreme groups and in the 2–8 desyatin group, but a decline in the other two groups.* It is therefore not possible on the sown area index to reach a definite conclusion. This is related to the fact that in the *volost'* there is a lot of fallow land which is much harder to improve (since it was closely connected to virgin land and thus rapidly returns to the wild) and requires two pairs of horses or oxen to plough any land, even soft land which is being ploughed again. Only three or four pairs make it possible to plough fully properly. Thus only farms with over 12 *desyatins (see Table 95)* have enough horses to plough even easy land, and in most cases the 2–8 *desyatins* group has insufficient working livestock to plough. Thus the growth registered in their number and their own area is to a significant degree based on taking on alien livestock. The above table also shows that the 'loading' of horses in the very highest sown area farms is lower than in the ones just below them. *Calculating the 'loading' per* desyatin *on horses for the different sown area groupings, Kritsman concluded that the very highest group (over 20* desyatins) *did not rent out horses, but took on hired wage-labour, whereas the groups of from 12–20* desyatins *hired out livestock to the groups with a lower sown area. Kritsman then turned to the distribution of farms grouped by working livestock:*

TABLE 96

PERCENTAGE OF FARMS WITH LIVESTOCK

	Without working livestock	With 1 head	With 2 head	With 3 head	With 4 head	With 5 head	With 6 head	Over 6 head	Total
Percentage of farms									
1923	28.3	24.6	17.7	12.8	6.1	6.3	1.9	2.3	100
1924	30.8	28.2	15.6	13.7	4.4	4.4	1.4	1.5	100
Percentage of livestock									
1923	—	13.3	18.9	20.9	13.2	17.1	6.4	10.2	100
1924	—	17.4	19.5	25.4	10.9	13.6	5.5	7.7	100
Percentage of sown area									
1923	12.4	16.5	17.6	16.7	10.5	13.9	5.1	7.3	100
1924	14.4	19.0	16.3	20.7	8.7	10.5	4.5	5.9	100

These figures seem to support the results for Shchuch'aya Station, giving a downward movement, but it is only a stage in the process of class stratification, as Table 97 also indicates.

Taking Tables 96 and 97 together, those with one or no horse have increased their sown area from 28.9 per cent in 1923 to 43.3 per cent in 1924. This requires the use of alien working livestock, and could thus be considered as the growth of the hidden sown area of the highest group. The sown area of farms with three head of working livestock could be considered partly as a growth of the sown area on the basis of the *supryaga (joint use of stock)* of farms of equal capacity, and partly the growth of sown area of powerful farms

TABLE 97

AVERAGE SOWN AREA WITHIN LIVESTOCK GROUPINGS

	Without working livestock	With 1 head	With 2 head	With 3 head	With 4 head	With 5 head	With 6 head	Over 6 head	Overall average
Average sown area per farm									
1923	1.1	1.6	2.4	3.1	4.1	5.3	6.1	7.9	2.4
1924	1.2	1.7	2.6	3.7	4.9	5.9	7.5	10.2	2.5
Average sown area per head									
1923	—	1.6	1.2	1.0	1.0	1.1	1.0	1.1 (or less)	—
1924	—	1.7	1.3	1.2	1.2	1.2	1.3	1.5 (or less)	—

which had for the time being sold a horse (to pay taxes, for example). The reduction in the sown area (and number of horses) among the highest livestock groups was thus partly offset by the growth in their hidden sown area. The livestock group went down proportionately less than the number of farms in that group. In other words, the surviving highest livestock farms concentrated more sown area and livestock in their hands, which is not evident simply from the classification of farms by livestock.

Finally, for this study, one can compare the percentage of farms without sown area and without working livestock:

TABLE 98

PERCENTAGE OF FARMS WITHOUT SOWN AREA AND WITHOUT WORKING LIVESTOCK: 1923–4

	Without sown area	Without working livestock	Excess of farms without livestock over farms without sown area	Percentage of sown area in farms without livestock	Average sown area per farm without livestock
1923	5.5	28.3	22.8	12.4	1.1
1924	6.0	30.8	24.8	14.4	1.2

There are no data on the hiring of livestock or stock, but the report says that the basic feature of stratification is working livestock, and that the poor peasant is compelled to hire under conditions that are quite heavy for him. There is no accurate count for the *volost'* of farms hiring in (or hiring out) labour power, but, according to local workers, in the working season no less than 25 per cent of farms hire in workers, which corresponds to the percentage of farms with 3 horses and more. It is reported that there were around 1,500 *batraki* in the *volost'*, which for 3,111 farms means one rural wage-worker for every two farms, and two *batraki* for every farm actually hiring wage-labour.

(ii) Aleksandrovskaya Volost', Kustanaiskaya Gubernia

This is taken from the article by A. Yermolenko of the Central Committee of the Russian Communist Party [*Yermolenko*, 1925]. It does not contain direct data on the dynamics of the class stratification of the peasantry. The report says that the ground is solid and needs four to five horses to a one-horse plough, and three to four horses on waste ground. Hence 70 per cent of the horseless and one-horse farms depend on the remaining 30 per cent with many horses. Usually the one-horse farms 'cooperate' (*jointly use the yoke*) with two- or three-horse farms, more rarely with other one-horse farms. In the majority of cases the form of exploitation is 'working off' in very varied ways, right up to the brewing by the poor peasant of home brew for the prosperous peasant. Ploughing is done almost exclusively with a plough, rather than, say, a *sokha* (*wooden plough*). In 1924 the distribution of peasant farms in terms of horses was as follows:

TABLE 99
GROUPING BY HORSES: 1924

	Without horses	With 1 head	With 2 head	With 3 head	With 4 head	With 5 head	Over 5 head	Total
Percentage of farms	35.6	35.1	20.0	5.8	2.1	1.0	0.4	100
Percentage of sown area	9.6	26.0	31.4	16.5	9.8	4.9	1.8	100
Shortage or surplus of grain in puds per farm	−17	+1.5	+63	+158	+260	+341	+259	—
Sown area per farm (*des.*)	1.37	3.13	6.62	11.99	19.71	20.18	18.00	—
Average per horse	—	3.13	3.31	4.00	4.93	4.04	<3.00	—

Thus, in a manner similar to the previous study, the 'loading' on one horse (and sown area) is slightly lower in the highest livestock farms, than in the group just below them. This is partly explained by the fact that the most prosperous peasants buy wheat in the villages, and own horses that are doing nothing in winter, and are hired out in summer. Thus the extra horses are not used on their own farms. Characteristically, only 17 per cent of farms without horses do not sow. There are farms sowing up to 70 *desyatins*, harvesting over 2,000 puds of grain. There are 170 registered *batraki*, averaging one to every three farms with two or more horses (and no less than one to every six farms living by 'working off').

Since it is similar to Shchuch'inskaya Volost', it is interesting to see the social composition of various kinds of rural organisations. On the direction of the cooperatives, it is reported that one was in the hands of the prosperous, one had three middle peasants running it (of whom one was a former local shopkeeper), the third was run by the poor, but its Auditing Commission was run by prosperous and middle peasants, and the fourth was directed by two poor peasants and one middle peasant. Defining the poor as those with one or no horse, the middle with two horses (although the report is not clear on this) and prosperous as those with three or more, the following table indicates access to school:

TABLE 100

	Poor	Middle	Prosperous
Percentage of farms	74	17	9
Percentage of children in school in autumn	41	29	30

Fifteen per cent of children of school age never study, mostly because of lack of footwear and clothing. During the summer 25 per cent of children, most of them poor, are absent. The following table shows the social composition of the *sel'sovety* of four (*or, in brackets, five*) villages:

TABLE 101
SOCIAL COMPOSITION OF RURAL SOVIETS

	Without horses	With 1 head	With 2 head	With 3 head	With 4 head	With 5 head	Over 5 head	Total
Percentage of all farms	36 (36)	37 (36)	19.5 (20)	5 (5)	2 (2)	0.3 (0.8)	0.2 (0.4)	100
Among members of rural Soviets	29	36	21	7	5	0.7	1.3	100
Percentage of farms with members in rural Soviets	9	11	12	14	29	25	67	—
Among the president and members of the praesidium	20 (15)	40 (31)	20 (15)	—	10 (15)	—	10 (23)	—
Percentage of farms with president or members of the praesidium	0.4 (0.4)	0.8 (0.8)	0.8 (0.7)	—	4.1 (6.7)	—	33.3 (50)	—

Three-quarters of the most prosperous farms have members in rural soviets, and one half are in the praesidium (as member or president). The author remarks that the contemporary Soviet people are to be found among the very prosperous peasants.[12] (*A similar conclusion could be reached on the basis of figures on membership of the Russian Communist Party in one village.*) Agricultural tax falls primarily on the poorest peasants; see Table 102.

This is a slightly misleading picture since the report takes the harvest per *desyatin* as the same. Consequently for the lowest group the gross harvest and surplus is exaggerated, and is reduced for the highest group. The translation of the tax into puds assumed a single price for all groups, while the author

TABLE 102

INCIDENCE OF TAXATION ON HARVEST

	Without horse, but with sown area	With 1 horse	With 2 horses	With 3 horses	With 4 horses	With 5 horses	With 6 and more horses
Gross harvest per farm	41.1	93.9	198.6	359.7	591.3	605.4	540
Surplus grain (after deducting seeds and family produce)	−13.7	18.3	99.5	219.8	371.8	402.5	330
Tax per farm (translated into puds)	3.6	16.9	36.9	61.5	112	61	71
As a percentage of the surplus	—	92	37	28	30	15	21
As a percentage of gross harvest	9	18	18	16	19	10	13
As a percentage of of all the tax	5	28	35	17	11	3	1

indicates that the poor receive 80 kopecks for their grain, while the rich get two roubles, so the tax for the rich is exaggerated by up to 2½ times. Thus one could truly say that in this *volost'* the prosperous actually pay a proportionately lower tax on their gross harvest than the horseless farm. The agricultural tax takes all the surplus of a one-horse farm, forcing them to work as *batraki* or by 'working off' for the prosperous. However, not only tax, but also state help to the poor (in the form of seed loans for sowing) sometimes becomes an instrument for the subordination of the poor by the prosperous, since it can be used as a means of payment to the prosperous, ending up among the two- and three-horse farms.

(iii) Tisul'skii Region, Tomsk Gubernia

Once again this is based on a document by a member of the Central Committee of the Russian Communist Party, A. Musatov. This one is unpublished. (*Even where there was a published version, Kritsman worked from longer unpublished documents.*) It contains data (from the *Gubstatburo*) on changes from 1922 to 1924 in working livestock and sown area, reproduced in the following two tables:

TABLE 103

PERCENTAGE OF FARMS WITH WORKING LIVESTOCK

	Without working livestock	With 1 head	With 2 head	With 3 head	With 4 head	Total
1922	3.82	20.61	40.84	18.70	16.03	100
1924	0.35	11.85	38.33	28.57	20.90	100

TABLE 104

PERCENTAGE OF FARMS WITH SOWN AREA

	1922	1924
Without sown area	0.76	0.35
Up to 1.1 *des.*	19.47	10.80
1.1–2.1 *des.*	22.14	17.77
2.1–3.1 *des.*	19.85	18.82
3.1–4.1 *des.*	17.17	19.51
4.1–6.1 *des.*	15.65	20.21
6.1–8.1 *des.*	1.91	7.32
8.1–10.1 *des.*	1.51	3.83
10.1–16.1 *des.*	1.90	1.39
Total	100.00	100.00

The report claims that these data are somewhat doubtful, since the *Gubstatburo* figures show no farms with more than four horses, yet there are many farms with more than six horses and even 20 or 30 farms (that is, less than one per cent) with more than 10 horses. The same could be said in relation to sown area. The author claims that in 1924 there were around 20 per cent (not 12) of farms with one horse, around 68–9 (not 67) per cent with two or three horses and 10–11 per cent (not 21) with four or more horses. The author claims that hidden sown area is a mass phenomenon in this region.

On this evidence the *kulaks* are an insignificant part of the population, so that along with hidden sown area there is hidden stratification! In a word, it is impossible to take the figures presented seriously. (*Kritsman in a footnote showed that other figures were no better – they were absurd for Siberian conditions.*) The report claims that the position of the rich is improving, and of the poor is deteriorating, but there is no evidence on how widely the rich exploit the poor since the peasantry simply hide the *kulaks*. If one defines the *kulak* as a peasant hiring wage-labour the whole year round, then the number of such *kulaks* is growing all the time, but in the region there are other forms by which the *kulaks* exploit the poor, such as:

(a) Paying for the use of machines. In this region, because of the very short and rainy summer and autumn, it is difficult without harvesting machinery to sow, harvest the grain and provide sufficient fodder for the livestock. Grain is threshed exclusively by a thresher. Wheat in the region is full of weeds, so a sorting machine is completely necessary. The rich rent out these machines. By the accounts verified by the commission of the *Sibrevkom* and well known to the peasants themselves, a thresher pays for itself in a year, as does a harvester. There are farms which have reduced their sown area or even stopped sowing and now live off their machinery. There are more than 30 such farms, that is, half of one per cent of the farms.

(b) Paying by 'working off' loan of grain, hay and so on. Such a form of payment is usually twice as dear to the peasant if one considers the cost of wage-labour.

(c) Renting out the best land. Often five or six of the rich use the best land, for 'help' with the grain or hay harvest. In 1923 this was because the poor could not afford to pay rent. Even the old *obshchina* (called 'love') is a form of exploitation. It widely and systematically uses free labour power, employing on an annual basis an entire village within its boundaries, whose members bring their own horses, plough, thresh and so on, and are paid worse rates than by the local *kulaks*. The *obshchina* pays between one quarter and one half of the rates paid by *kulaks*, depending on the task.

The political influence of the prosperous is also growing in the region: the numbers of prosperous peasants (with four or more horses) on the praesidium of the *sel'sovet* has grown from two to five. Four peasants were elected to the Regional Executive Committee, all very rich, and poor and *batrak* candidates are often removed. The *batraki* do not go to the *sel'sovet* because they are not peasants. Where there is a clash of groups, the prosperous are the deciders.

PRELIMINARY CONCLUSIONS

The data have not been artificially selected. I have used all the material available to me. Despite problems of generalising from the data (they are small-scale studies, although covering the main regions of the USSR), one can draw out from the data definite methods of approach to a greater mass of material. Only on the basis of the latter will it be possible to arrive at definite conclusions on the problems indicated, in further works. Nevertheless, it is possible to draw certain preliminary conclusions:

1. Until now the basic growing form of capitalist agriculture in the USSR has been the capitalist agriculture (predominantly petty-capitalist) based on the hiring out of working livestock and agricultural stock, under which the hidden capitalist appears as a worker, working on someone else's farm with his own working livestock and stock, and the hidden proletarian appears as an owner without working livestock or without stock (or with insufficient livestock and stock) hiring the possessor of these indispensable means or production. The 'hirer' pays by 'working off' on the farm of the person hired, which often leaves insufficient wages to the 'hirer'. Whether the 'hired' peasant works on the farm of the hirer does not change the essence of the matter. In these relations, capitalist appropriation of surplus value is not created by the labour of the hired 'worker' with his horse and stock, but by the labour of the hiring 'boss'; the labour of the latter becomes possible only because the means of production of the hired man are used on his farm. In some areas this form of exploitation covers 70 to 75 per cent of peasant farms (the South East and the Ukraine). The hidden sown area has gone up to 30 or 40 per cent of the total sown area (in Tambov and the South East). In some regions the hiring of livestock predominates: the South East, Siberia, the Central Agricultural Region, areas of grain production. In others, the hiring of stock predominates: the Ukraine, the

Industrial Centre, and generally regions of industrial crops and livestock rearing. The recording of this kind of capitalist development is entirely unsatisfactory. Having sown area without livestock or stock leads to a subordinate role. The *supryaga* (*literally yoking or harnessing together, sometimes called the* spryaga) is often a cover for the hiring of working livestock and stock, depending on the different 'strengths' of the farms involved. Where there is equal strength, in some conditions it is an embryo of collective agriculture.

2. There also exists the usual type of capitalism, based on the hiring of rural wage-workers. It also appears to a small degree in covert form: every sort of fictitious family relationship serves as a screen. This is a quite widely dispersed phenomenon in the Soviet countryside, judging by statements in the press, yet doubtless most cases pass undetected. Even when not covert, rural wage-labour is often not registered: daily wage-labour is completely unregistered, despite Lenin's analysis of a quarter of a century ago indicating that the hiring of day labourers is to the greatest degree the characteristic sign of the peasant bourgeoisie. This increased significantly after the Revolution. Finally, the statistical registration of time-rate hiring of wage-labour is to the greatest degree unsatisfactory, so the increase in wage-labour might to a certain extent be simply due to better recording.

3. Besides these two forms of capitalist economy, which are the forms of action of industrial capital,[13] for in both these forms capital acts as the owner of means used in production, there are also forms of trading and usury capital whose activity in the countryside is widespread. The basis of usury capital is the instability of the majority of peasant farms, whereas the basis of trading capital is the monopoly of connections with the market (lack of working livestock). Usury and trading capital are also interlinked, in that trading operations are, to a growing extent in rural life, connected with credit. Frequently usury and manufacturing capital are similarly interlinked. The widely dispersed phenomenon of advances of grain is accompanied by the unpaid 'working off' on the farm of the lender. This is in effect a form of interest on the loan, although they would claim they make no profit out of it. There is a lack of recording of trading and especially usury capital.

4. The state apparatus operates in the same direction as trading, usury and manufacturing capital, by the pressure of its taxes. It forces the poor to bring their labour power on to the market. This situation might have changed somewhat with the removal of the tax burden on the poor and on 35 per cent of peasant farms in general, since the studies were conducted.[14]

5. The prosperous (capitalists and those becoming capitalists) are, as well as the collectives, the bearers of progress in agriculture. (*In an interesting footnote giving a critique of the un-named ideologues of the petit-bourgeoisie, Kritsman nevertheless pointed out that capitalist farms were reactionary in Soviet conditions.*) Capitalist farms more than all the others use technical (agrotechnical and other) improvements, engage in agricultural cooperation, use the Soviet school and so on. They tend to gain influence on the *sel'sovety,*

their praesidiums, the *Volost'* Executive Committee and the apparatus of local power, and appear as the leaders of the whole peasantry.

6. An index of the growth of the economic power of the capitalist part of the peasantry is the growth of rented land, relieving the poor of the land they received as a result of the second stage of the agricultural revolution, the Committees of the Poor. The prosperous rent in the land rented out by the state, but renting in of land often takes the form of hiring out working livestock and stock.

7. The growth of the class stratification does not occur as the stratification by land, but as stratification by working livestock. In so far as it occurs in a hidden form, it is disguised as equalisation in terms of sown area. Livestock and stock are the border dividing the proletarian from the petit-bourgeois, but these indices do not distinguish among the peasantry with the means to conduct their own farm; in particular they do not characterise differences in the capitalist peasantry, because of the many sided character of capital.

8. The growth of class stratification is not only the growth in the numbers of lowest and highest groups, but in terms of the average means of production of these groups. There has been an absolute and relative decline in means of production among the lowest peasants, and an absolute (and sometimes only relative) growth in the means of production of the highest groups; that is, a concentration of the means of production in the highest groups.

9. In the latter cases, similar changes in the possession of the means of production characterise the *hidden* phases in the class stratification of the peasantry, for the class stratification (differentiation) of the peasantry occurs *dialectically;* quite often in the form of the so-called movement downwards and movement upwards, including in it, as its own phases, a phase mainly of destruction (in all sown area or other groupings) of the weak farms, and then a phase mainly of increase of the strong farms.

10. The process of class stratification takes different forms in connection with the ruling commodity direction of peasant farming (grain, special crops, dairy farming and so on) and proceeds basically by means of commodity peasant farming. This has *radical* significance for the industrial (and several other) regions. In so far as grain production has a consumptionist character, based on the domestic farms of wage-labourers or small farms engaged in non-cultivating activities, or cultivating non-grain crops, then *grouping by sown area is fundamentally grouping by the extent of the domestic farm,* in which, generally speaking, the influence of capitalist differentiation is not present (for example, in the farms of industrial workers or town artisans). Where some farms are engaged in these regions in *commodity* grain production, then general data on *all* peasant farms gives a weak or even an unclear picture of the class differentiation of peasant farming. For this reason, the *consumptionist* peasant household (in essence the *domestic* farm of an essentially proletarian peasantry) requires special investigation.

These conclusions need wider material, better prepared for this purpose in future. One must also draw attention to the other processes besides capitalist differentiation: the cooperative unification of small farms (*at the time only one or 1.5 per cent of them, although in a footnote added in 1928 Kritsman pointed to the speeding up of this process).* All commodity farms are being drawn in by the many sided aspects of cooperation, into the general system of the Soviet national economy, with large-scale agriculture already in the hands of the proletariat (*sovkhozy*). Finally, there is the increase in the mass of active middle peasants, as well as capitalist differentiation, the middle peasantry no longer being the objects of feudal exploitation. All these processes are influencing and being influenced by the process of capitalist development. Without taking them into account, it is impossible to arrive at a correct judgement as to where the Soviet countryside is going.

One can conclude this translation of one of Kritsman's earlier works by stressing that the tentative nature of its conclusions is not indicative of a failure to develop an adequate strategy for the socialist transformation of the countryside. Rather it is indicative of an awareness of the need for careful research, taking account of differences in the technical division of labour and the division of social production, into the different forms of development of capitalist and socialist relations of production, before refining a strategy taken over in broad outline from Lenin.

TRANSLATOR'S NOTES TO KRITSMAN

1. This distinction by Kritsman amounts to a distinction between the determinants of the process of differentiation, on the one hand, and the categorisation of individual farms as capitalist, proletarian or 'middle', on the other.

2. The phrase 'class stratification' carries the connotation of stratification as a process, rather than a settled state of affairs. For some reason, Kritsman seemed reluctant to use the word 'differentiation'.

3. On pages 141–6 of *Class Stratification,* Kritsman provides a critique of data on wage labour, using Ts.S.U. figures on Tula Gubernia. He argues that the figures are inaccurate, reflecting juridical relations, not economic ones. In particular they refer to permanent time-rate wage-labour, ignoring, say, day wage-labour or seasonal wage-labour. It is in a footnote on page 144 that there is reference to Lenin's conception of a worker with an allotment. There is further discussion of wage-labour where there are data on it in the individual surveys which he analysis later in *Class Stratification.* But it is clear even from the discussion on pages 141–6 that Kritsman does not treat wage-labour as a unitary phenomenon: it is related to the organisational forms of 'enterprise' occurring in the process of development of capitalism, and thus to hidden forms of capitalist exploitation. Hence Shanin's remarks on wage-labour seem to be misdirected; Kritsman [1929], Shanin [1972: 60–61].

4. In my view this approach enables one to take into consideration various determinants of relations of production, including various aspects of the division of labour, thus avoiding reliance on a single 'principle of stratification'.

5. Grosskopf is careful to point out that in 1916 there were evidently large properties which could properly be called capitalist, but that in the black earth zone, where in 1917 two-thirds of large properties possessed more than 500 *desyatins,* the mixed type of enterprise was the most frequent: a capitalist organisation of the enterprise and a feudal organisation of peasants co-existed. See S.M. Shipley [1979] for the historical background (up to the end of the 19th century) of this geographical distribution of forms of enterprise.

6. The *gubernii* containing the *volosti* analysed by Kritsman are outlined with a continuous line, and their names are underlined in the list of *gubernii* below the map. In addition, the Don *gubernia,* where the six *sel'sovety* used in Kritsman's critique of the 'banal' approach were located, is also outlined on this map. It is geographically close to the South East Study.

7. Kritsman's calculations of the percentage changes over the years are not presented here. I have corrected misprints.

8. 'Station' in the context means a large village.

9. The rates of pay by the poor farm for this form of the *spryaga,* where the prosperous peasant used his means of production on the poor farm, can be indicated by the following examples:
    1. For ploughing and harvesting of one *desyatin* – two workers (from the poor farm working on the prosperous farm) for the whole harvest and threshing.
    2. For ploughing and harvesting – 50 per cent of the harvested grain.
    3. For ploughing ½ *desyatin* – a youth working for the whole summer (on the prosperous farm).
    4. For sowing three *desyatins* – 50 per cent of the harvest and one worker for 18 days.
    5. For ploughing and harvesting three *desyatins* – two workers for almost the whole summer.

10. This is consistent with the impression given by the note on *promysly* by R.E.F. Smith [1975]. Smith is discussing primarily the use of the term in relation to an earlier note by Shanin [1975]. Both Shanin and Smith are aware that at times *promysly* refers to wage-labour.

11. According to my calculations, the undersampling for 1917 was 9.2 per cent, but as I have indicated before, there are few misprints or arithmetical errors in Kritsman's work. Table 62 is thus slightly misleading for the 1917 number of farms, but there is no reason to doubt the sown area figure.

12. This corroborates the analysis of the *sel'sovet* given for the period up to about 1926 by M. Lewin [1968: 81–4]. Lewin points out, of course, the spectacular change in policy towards the *sel'sovet* in 1929.

13. *Promyshlenny* is probably used here in the sense of *promysly,* referring to handicraft or artisanal production, rather than machine production.

14. As argued in 'The Agrarian Marxist Research in its Political Context. . .' (see above Part II), the effect of taxation was not only, or perhaps even primarily, to force the poor to sell their labour power. It also forced them to market their grain, and in the existing conditions was often the only motive for doing so.

Bibliography

Anisimov, Yu. A., Vermenichev, I., Naumov, K., 1927, *Proizvodstvennaya kharakteristika krest'yanskikh khozyaistv razlichnykh sotsial'nykh grupp,* Moscow.

Arutyunyan, Yu. V., 1971, *Sotsial'naya struktura sel'skogo naseleniya SSSR,* Moscow.

Bettelheim, C., 1976, *Class Struggles in the USSR: First Period,* London.

Bettelheim, C., 1978, *Class Struggles in the USSR: Second Period,* London.

Bettelheim, C., Chavance, B., 1981, 'Stalinism as the Idealogy of State Capitalism', *Review of Radical Political Economics,* Vol. 13, No. 1.

Bolshakov, A. M., 1925, *Sovetskaya derevnya za 1917–25gg.,* Leningrad.

Carr, E. H., 1970, *Socialism in One Country,* Harmondsworth.

Carr, E. H., Davies, R. W., 1969, *Foundations of a Planned Economy,* Vol. 1, London.

Chagin, B. A., 1971, *Ocherk istorii sotsiologicheskoi mysli v SSSR,* Leningrad.

Chayanov, A. V., 1915, *Byudzhety krest'yan Starobelskogo uezda,* Kharkov.

Chayanov, A. V., 1925, *Organizatsiya krest'yanskogo khozyaistva,* Moscow. (Translated into English as 'Peasant Farm Organisation' in Thorner et al. (eds.), [1966].)

Cox, T. M., 1979a, *Rural Sociology in the Soviet Union,* London.

Cox, T. M., 1979b, 'Awkward Class or Awkward Classes? Class Relations in the Russion Peasantry Before Collectivisation', *The Journal of Peasant Studies,* Vol. 7, No. 1.

Davies, R. W., 1970, 'A Note on Grain Statistics', *Soviet Studies,* Vol. XXI, No. 3.

Ennew, J., Hirst, P., and Tribe, K., 1977, ' "Peasantry" as an Economic Category', *The Journal of Peasant Studies,* Vol. 4, No. 4.

Gaister, A. I., 1927a, 'Arenda i sdacha zemli', *Na Agrarnom Fronte,* No. 6.

Gaister, A. I., 1927b, 'Sootnoshenie klassov i grupp v derevne', *Na Agrarnom Fronte,* No. 10.

Gaister, A. I., 1927c, 'Rassloenie derevni i oppositsiya', *Na Agrarnom Fronte,* No. 11–12.

Gaister, A. I., 1928a, *Rassloenie sovetskoi derevni,* Moscow.

Gaister, A. I., 1928b, 'Diskussiya o klassovykh gruppirovkakh krest'yanskikh khozyaistv', *Na Agrarnom Fronte,* No. 6–7.

Grosskopf, S., 1976, *L'alliance ouvriere et paysanne en URSS (1921–28). Le probleme du ble,* Paris.

Harrison, M., 1975, 'Chayanov and the Economics of the Russian Peasantry', *The Journal of Peasant Studies,* Vol. 2, No. 4.

Harrison, M., 1977a, 'Resource Allocation and Agrarian Class Formation', *The Journal of Peasant Studies,* Vol. 4, No. 2.

Harrison, M., 1977b, 'The Peasant Mode of Production in the Work of A. V. Chayanov', *The Journal of Peasant Studies,* Vol. 4, No. 4.

Harrison, M., 1978a, 'The Soviet Economy in the 1920s and 1930s', *Capital and Class,* No. 5.

Harrison, M., 1978b, Review of Solomon 1977, *The Journal of Peasant Studies,* Vol. 6, No. 1.

Harrison, M., 1979, 'Chayanov and the Marxists', *The Journal of Peasant Studies,* Vol. 7, No. 1.

Hindess, B. (ed.), 1977, *Sociological Theories of the Economy,* London.

Hobsbawn, E., *et al.,* 1980, *Peasants in History,* Oxford.

Humphrey, C., 1974, 'Inside a Mongolian Tent', *New Society,* 31 October.

Humphrey, C., 1978, 'Pastoral Nomadism in Mongolia: The Role of Herdsmen's Cooperatives in the National Economy', *Development and Change,* Vol. 9.

Humphrey, C., 1979, 'The Uses of Genealogy: A Historical Study of the Nomadic and Sedentarised Buryat', in *Pastoral Production and Society,* Cambridge, 1979.

Hussain, A., Tribe, K., 1981, *Marxism and the Agrarian Question,* (2 vols.) London.

Jasny, N., 1972, *Soviet Economists of the Twenties,* Cambridge.

Karcz, J., 1967, 'Thoughts on the Grain Problem', *Soviet Studies,* Vol. XVIII, No. 4.

Karcz, J., 1970, 'Back on the Grain Front', *Soviet Studies,* Vol. XXII, No. 2.

Khryashcheva, A. I., 1926, *Gruppy i klassy v krest'yanstve,* Moscow.

Krest'yanskoe, 1923, *Krest'yanskoe khozyaistvo za vremya revolyutsii,* Moscow.

Kretov, F., 1925, *Derevnya posle revolyutsii,* Moscow.

Kritsman, L. N., 1921a, *Obshchestvennyi trud rabochego i edinolichnyi semeinyi trud krest'yanina,* Moscow.

Kritsman, L. N., 1921b, *O edinom khozyaistvennom plane,* Moscow.

Kritsman, L. N., 1922, 'O russkoi revolyutsii', *Vestnik Sotsialisticheskoi Akademii,* No. 1.

Kritsman, L. N., 1923a, 'Krupnoe i melkoe khozyaistvo v zemledelii', *Vestnik Sotsialisticheskoi Akademii,* No. 3, republished in Kritsman [1929c].

Kritsman, L. N., 1923b, 'O nakoplenii kapitala i "tretikh" litsakh', *Vestnik Sotsialisticheskoi Akademii,* No. 5.

Kritsman, L. N., 1923c, 'Ot tyagi k zemle k tyage k rynku', *Sotsialisticheskoe Khozyaistvo,* No. 4–5, republished in Kritsman [1929c].

Kritsman, L. N., 1924a, 'Sel'skoe khozyaistvo v sisteme narodnogo khozyaistva v pervye tri goda novoi ekonomicheskoi politiki', in a pamphlet, *Tri goda novoi ekonomicheskoi politiki,* Moscow, republished in Kritsman [1929c].

Kritsman, L. N., 1924b, 'Sovremennaya melko-burzhuaznaya politicheskaya ekonomiya', *Vestnik Kommunisticheskoi Akademii,* No. 7, also published as the foreword to Chayanov [1924b] and in Kritsman [1929c]. (Page references to Chayanov, 1924b.)

Kritsman, L. N., 1925a, 'Arifmetika i znanie dela (o trudakh zemplana i o professorakh Kondratieve i Oganovskom)', *Na Agrarnom Fronte,* No. 1.

Kritsman, L. N., 1925b, *Geroicheskii period russkoi revolyutsii,* Moscow, also published in *Vestnik Kommunisticheskoi Akademii,* No. 9, 1924.

Kritsman, L. N., 1925c, 'Kolkhoznoe dvizhenie (o ego literaturnom otrazhenii)', republished in Kritsman [1929c].

Kritsman, L. N., 1925d, 'K voprosu o klassovom rassloenii sovremennoi derevni', in four parts, respectively in *Na Agrarnom Fronte,* Nos. 2, 7–8, 9, 10.

Kritsman, L. N., 1925e, 'Lenin i put k sotsializmu', *Na Agrarnom Fronte,* No. 3, paper delivered to the Communist Academy, 24 January 1925, republished in Kritsman [1929c].

Kritsman, L. N., 1925f, 'Ob osnovakh perspektivnogo plana razvitiya sel'skogo i lesnogo khozyaistva', *Na Agrarnom Fronte,* No. 7–8.

Kritsman, L. N., 1925g, 'Perezhitki ideologii krepostnichestva v nashei statistike', *Na Agrarnom Fronte,* No. 1, republished in Kritsman [1929c].

Kritsman, L. N., 1925h, 'Plan sel'skogo khozyaistva i industrializatsiya' paper presented to the presidium of Gosplan in 1925, republished in Kritsman [1929c].

Kritsman, L. N., 1925i, 'Soyuz proletariata i bol'shinstva krest'yanstva v SSSR posle pobedy revolyutsii', *Bolshevik,* No. 2, republished in Kritsman [1929c].

Kritsman, L. N., 1925j, 'Stikhiya oproberzheniya i ee zherta (po povodu pisma prof. Oganovskogo)', *Na Agrarnom Fronte,* No. 2.

Kritsman, L. N., 1926a, 'Klassovaya differentsiatsiya krest' yanstva v sovremennoi sovetskoi derevne', *Vestnik Kommunisticheskoi Akademii,* No. 14, republished in Kritsman [1929c]. (Page numbers refer to 1929c.)

Kritsman, L. N., 1926b, *Klassovoe rassloenie sovetskoi derevni (po dannym volostnykh obsledovanii),* Moscow, republished in Kritsman [1929c].

Kritsman, L. N., 1926c, 'Razvitie kapitalizma i progress tekhniki', *Vestnik Kommunisticheskoi Akademii,* No. 16.

Kritsman, L. N., 1926–7, 'O statisticheskom izuchenii klassovoi struktury sovetskoi derevni', *Na Agrarnom Fronte,* Nos. 2, 1926; 7, 1927; 8–9, 1927; 10, 1927; republished in Kritsman [1929c].

Kritsman, L. N., 1927a, "Desyat' let na agrarnom fronte proletarskoi revolyutsii", *Na Agrarnom Fronte,* No. 11–12, republished in Kritsman [1929c].

Kritsman, L. N., 1927b, *Novy etap. (K proektam 'Obshchikh nachal zemlepol'zovaniya i zemleustroistva'),* republished in Kritsman [1929c].

Kritsman, L. N., 1928a, 'Klassovye gruppirovki krest'yanskikh khozyaistv', *Na Agrarnom Fronte,* No. 4, paper presented to the Communist Academy, January 1928, republished in Kritsman [1929c].

Kritsman, L. N. (ed.), 1928b, *Materialy po istorii agrarnoi revolyutsii,* Vol. 1, Moscow.

Kritsman, L. N., 1928c, 'Ob analize klassovoi struktury krest'yanstva', introduction to Gaister [1928a], republished in Kritsman [1929c].

Kritsman, L. N., 1928d, 'O samarskom obsledovanii', foreword to Vermenichev et al., [1928], republished in Kritsman [1929c].

Kritsman, L. N., 1929a, 'Ob osnovnykh metodakh razrabotki massovykh statisticheskikh materialov nashei agrarnoi revolyutsii', in Kritsman [1929c].

Kritsman, L. N., 1929b, 'O vnutrennikh protivorechiyakh krest'yanskogo dvora', introduction to Kubanin, 1929, republished in Kritsman [1929c].

Kritsman, L. N., 1929c, *Proletarskaya revolyutsiya i derevnya,* Moscow-Leningrad.

Kritsman, L. N., 1930a, Biography of Kritsman in *Malaya Sovetskaya Entsiklopediya,* Vol. 4.

Kritsman, L. N., 1930b, 'The Process of Socialisation of Agriculture in the U.S.S.R.', *Proceedings of the Conference of Agricultural Economists,* New York.

Kritsman, L. N., 1930c, 'O kharaktere nashei revolyutsii', *Na Agrarnom Fronte,* No. 4.

Lampert, N., 1979, *The Technical Intelligentsia and the Soviet State,* London.

Lenin, V. I., 1899, *The Development of Capitalism in Russia,* (reprinted according to the text of the 2nd (1908) edition in Lenin, *Collected Works,* Vol. 3, Moscow, 1964).

Lenin, V. I., 1921, *The Tax in Kind,* (reprinted in Lenin, *Collected Works,* Vol. 32, Moscow, 1965).

Lenin, V. I., 1923, *On Cooperation,* (reprinted in Lenin, *Collected Works,* Vol. 33, Moscow, 1966).

Lewin, M., 1968, *Russian Peasants and Soviet Power,* London.

Lezhnev-Finkovskii, T., Savchenko, K., 1925, *Kak zhivyet derevnya,* Moscow.

Litso, 1925, *Litso Donskoi derevni,* Rostov on Don.

Littlejohn, G.,1973a, 'The Peasantry and the Russian Revolution', *Economy and Society,* Vol. 2, No. 1.

Littlejohn, G., 1973b, 'The Russian Peasantry: A Reply to Teodor Shanin', *Economy and Society,* Vol. 2, No. 3.

Littlejohn, G., 1977, 'Chayanov and the Theory of Peasant Economy', in Hindess (ed.) [1977].

Littlejohn, G., 1979, 'State, Plan and Market in the Transition to Socialism: the Legacy of Bukharin', *Economy and Society,* Vol. 8, No. 2.
Littlejohn, G., 1984, *A Sociology of the Soviet Union,* Basingstoke.
Miliband, R., 1975, 'Bettelheim and the Soviet Experience', *New Left Review,* No. 91.
Morosanov, A., Yermolenko, E., 1925, 'Akmolinskaya derevnya', *Na Agrarnom Fronte,* Nos. 7–8, 9.
Morrison, D., 1982, 'A Critical Examination of A. A. Barsov's Empirical Work on the Balance of Value Exchanges Between Town and Country', *Soviet Studies,* Vol. XXXIV, No. 4.
Naumov, K. I., 1928, 'Problema differentsiatsii krest'yanskikh khozyaistv', *Puti Sel'skogo Khozyaistva,* No. 4–5.
Naumov, K. I., Shardin, D., 1928, 'Opyt postroeniya klassovoi gruppirovki krest'yanskikh khozyaistv', *Na Agrarnom Fronte, No. 4.*
Nemchinov, V. S., 1926a, 'Zadachi statistiki v svyazi s resheniem III sessii oblispolkoma', *Byulleten' Uralskogo Oblastnogo Statisticheskogo Upravleniya,* No. 1, reprinted in Nemchinov [1967].
Nemchinov, V. S., 1926b, 'O statisticheskom izuchenii klassovogo rassloeniya derevni', *Buylleten' Uralskogo Oblastnogo Statisticheskogo Upravleniya,* No. 1, reprinted in Nemchinov [1967].
Nemchinov, V. S., 1927a, 'O sotsial'no-ekonomicheskikh gruppirovkakh krest'yanskikh khozyaistv', *Vsesoyuznoe Statisticheskoe Soveshchanie 1927 goda,* Moscow. Reprinted in Nemchinov [1967].
Nemchinov, V. S., 1927b, 'Programma i organizatsiya dinamicheskikh perepisei', *Vsesoyuznoe Statisticheskoe Soveshchanie 1927 goda,* Moscow. Reprinted in Nemchinov [1967].
Nemchinov, V. S., 1928a, 'Opyt klassifikatsii krest'yanskikh khozyaistv', *Vestnik Statistiki,* No. 1, reprinted in Nemchinov [1967].
Nemchinov, V. S., 1928b, 'Diskussiya o klassovykh gruppirovkakh krest'yanskikh khozyaistv', *Na Agrarnom Fronte,* No. 8.
Nemchinov, V. S., 1967, *Izbrannye proizvedeniya,* tom 1, Moscow.
Nove, A., 1964, *Was Stalin Really Necessary?* London.
Popov, A., 1928, Review of Gaister 1928a, *Planovoe Khozyaistvo,* No. 4.
Preobrazhenskii, E. A., 1926, *Novaya ekonomika,* (translated as *The New Economics,* Oxford, 1965).
Shanin, T., 1972, *The Awkward Class,* Oxford.
Shanin, T., 1973, 'Gary Littlejohn's Review of T. Shanin, *The Awkward Class',* *Economy and Society,* Vol. 2, No. 2.
Shanin, T., 1975, 'Promysly', *The Journal of Peasant Studies,* Vol. 2, No. 2.
Shipley, S. M., 1979, *The Sociology of the Peasantry, Populism and the Russian Peasant Commune,* M. Phil. thesis, University of Lancaster.
Smith, K., 1979, 'Introduction to Bukharin: Economic Theory and the Closure of the Soviet Industrialisation Debate', *Economy and Society,* Vol. 8, No. 4.

Smith, R. E. F., 1975, 'Crafts and Trades', *The Journal of Peasant Studies,* Vol. 2, No. 4.

Solomon, S. G., 1975, 'Controversy in Social Science: Soviet Rural Studies in the 1920s, *Minerva,* No. 13.

Solomon, S. G., 1977, *The Soviet Agrarian Debate: A Controversy in Social Science 1923–1929,* Boulder, Colorado.

Sulkovskii, M., 1930, *Klassovye gruppy i proizvodstvennye tipy krest'yanskikh khozyaistv,* Moscow.

Thorner, D., Kerblay, B., Smith, R. E. F. (eds.), 1966, *Chayanov: The Theory of Peasant Economy,* Homewood, Illinois.

Vermenichev, I., Gaister, A., Raevich, G., 1928, *710 khozyaistv Samarskoi derevni,* Moscow.

Vishnevskii, N., 1925, 'Novaya statisticheskaya literatura po sel'skomu i krest'yanskomu khozyaistvu', *Na Agrarnom Fronte,* Nos. 4, 5–6, 9, 10.

Yakovlev, Ya., 1923, *Derevnya kak ona est. Ocherki Nikolskoi volosti,* Moscow–Leningrad.

Yakovlev, Ya., 1924, *Nasha derevnya. Novoe v starom i staroe v novom,* Moscow–Leningrad. (2nd edition 1925).

Yakovlev, Ya., 1926, *Ob oshibakh khlebo-furazhnogo balansa Ts.S.U. i ego istolkovatelei,* Moscow.

Yancheskii, N. L. (ed.), 1924, *Kak zhivyet i chem boleet derevnya,* Rostov on Don.

Yermolenko, A., 1925, 'Kazakhstanskaya derevnya', *Na Agrarnom Fronte,* No. 9.

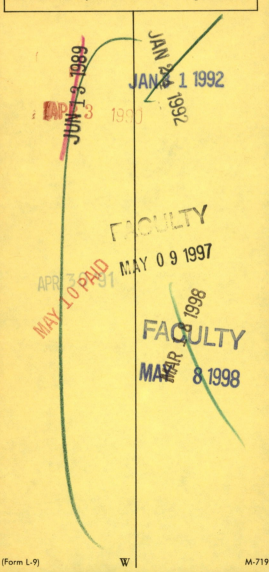